Deconstruction and the Ethical Turn

Deconstruction and the Ethical Turn

Peter Baker

University Press of Florida

Gainesville/Tallahassee/Tampa/Boca Raton
Pensacola/Orlando/Miami/Jacksonville

00 99 98 97 96 95 6 5 4 3 2 1

Library of Congress Cataloging-in-Publication Data

Baker, Peter, 1995–
    Deconstruction and the ethical turn / Peter Baker.
    p. cm.
    Includes bibliographical references (p.) and index.
    ISBN 0-8130-1365-8
    1. Deconstruction. I. Title.
  PN98.D43B35   1995   95-5313
  801'.95—dc20   CIP

The University Press of Florida is the scholarly publishing agency for the State
University System of Florida, comprised of Florida A & M University, Florida
Atlantic University, Florida International University, Florida State University,
University of Central Florida, University of Florida, University of North Florida,
University of South Florida, and University of West Florida.

University Press of Florida
15 Northwest 15th Street
Gainesville, FL 32611

To Debbie

Contents

Preface

The title of this study, *Deconstruction and the Ethical Turn*, is intended to rhyme with that movement in twentieth-century philosophy and literary theory called "the linguistic turn." As I discuss more fully in the introduction, this linguistic turn has widely been seen as establishing an attention to the underlying structure of language in any discourse of the human sciences. What I propose in this study is that the larger or more far-reaching effect of this turn is *not* to displace all decisions and actions into the linguistic field, but rather to see "writing" in the expanded sense given by Jacques Derrida in *Of Grammatology*, for example, as allowing an increased descriptive efficacy and transformative power to analyses of a wide array of human actions and fields of knowledge. This can already be seen in the effects of the movement known as deconstruction in fields as diverse as composition theory, architecture, and legal studies. My goal here is not to explore all the ramifications of the radical insights offered by deconstructive approaches into these various fields, or even to explore the literary critical dimensions of deconstruction. Rather, the approach I take here is to examine the significant texts and some of the related work undertaken by mainly French theorists and their American commentators. Deconstruction has so thoroughly entered the academic fields and the general or popular understanding that use of the term itself, like an earlier term, *existentialism*, is not limited to university professors and students but can be found in newspaper op-ed pages and even—who knows?—insults shouted by cab drivers. At such a point, a study such as this one may have the value of insisting on the seriousness of the deconstructive enterprise, its philosophical background, and its possible usefulness for negotiating the political terrain of the postmodern university, not to say the world.

In the introduction, I present a fuller version of the above story, presenting the crucial works by Derrida and Michel Foucault from the late sixties as a key turning point from structuralism/poststructuralism to an enlarged and very powerful critique of existing institutions of knowledge and human endeavor. In the first chapter, I attend to a form that the resistance to deconstruction takes—accusing Derrida of denying reference and of philosophical nihilism— in a representative recent text by Robert Scholes. I then attempt a limited explanation of the reasons for my focus on the work of Derrida rather than on the work of Foucault. I finally examine the work of Christopher Norris as an example of a critic who wants to insist on the continuing real-world efficacy of the deconstructive project. By examining critically some of Norris's affiliative scenarios, I indicate some of the limits of such an appropriative endeavor. In a sense, then, my own goal here is not to appropriate but to present an evaluation. Part of this presentational strategy consists in a roughly chronological ordering to the following chapters. The second chapter examines a key juncture from the early sixties between the philosophy of Maurice Merleau-Ponty and Jacques Lacan. I see Merleau-Ponty's phenomenology as a strong continuing influence on figures such as Lacan and Derrida, and Lacan's shift of Merleau-Ponty's insights into the intersubjective realm of affective relations and personal identity as a means of maintaining some of phenomenology's ethical force. The third chapter examines a similar juncture in the philosophy of difference by examining the philosophy of Martin Heidegger, the radicalizing moves of Gilles Deleuze, and the deconstructive breach of Derrida in relation to these two thinkers. The fourth chapter insists on the link between the deconstructive project of Derrida and the ethical philosophy of Emmanuel Levinas. I see Levinas's strong formulation of ethical *exteriority* as providing a guiding model for thinking the ethical turn as a turn outward toward others, responding to the call of the other. Similarly, the fifth chapter presents the critical theory of Julia Kristeva in the psychoanalytical and theoretical area as a version of ethical feminism. The sixth chapter investigates Derrida's work since the *Grammatology* in this context of thinking the ethical subject of discourse as an aspect of deconstruction's "impossible" ethics. My claim here is that Derrida's work has changed over time in a way to bring him closer to Levinas's ethical philosophy. In the final chapter I examine what I call Derrida's "negative" autobiography, especially the ways these texts situate the utterance in a context that highlights their singularity.

This is not, then, primarily an introductory approach to Derrida and the theory of deconstruction. I have come to see serious limitations with the whole idea of introducing the difficult materials associated with contemporary critical theory. Paradoxically, students not only desire to learn this field about which they have heard so much, they are also startlingly open to the most radical insights into human institutions, especially those of higher learning, that can be generated through in-depth discussions of the most difficult texts by Derrida, Foucault, and others. The ethical turn I see at work in these theoretical texts and in the ways they offer us of understanding our social formations is thus far from being an abstract concept. The ongoing activity of teaching, studying, analyzing, and discussing texts in a classroom is paradigmatic of the deconstructive mode generally, if I can offer something like a general statement. That is to say, institutions and other social formations (law, education, politics, economics, religion, and so on) not only can be deconstructed, but the wide area exposed by "writing," as used by Derrida, offers ways of performing (deconstructive) interpretive acts that are also transformative, and thus ethical, whether Derrida wants to insist on this last characterization or not.

There may be some readers who are disappointed that I do not attempt to read more traditional literary texts, or who feel that the various theoretical points raised would gain resonance from such a conjunction. *The Ethical Turn* is the twin, or double, of my earlier book from the University Press of Florida, *Obdurate Brilliance: Exteriority and the Modern Long Poem* (1991), where I examine the poetry of Saint-John Perse, Ezra Pound, Charles Olson, and others, using the model of *exteriority* that I most fully develop here in chapter 4.

The work on this book received institutional support from the Faculty Research Committee of Towson State University. Among the many people who have shared my interest in these subjects are some I want to thank explicitly. I especially want to express my gratitude to Albert Cook for his close attention to this work and for his deep and abiding friendship. I also want to thank Michael Ruby, David Bergman, Gary Handwerk, Vara Neverow, Tony Rosso, James Harding, Friederike Eigler, Carolyn Hill, Jo-Ann Pilardi, Scott Allen, Paul Miers, Linda Mahin,

Elaine Hedges, Beth Vanfossen, and Trent Owings, who all at one time or another commented on and responded to this work. I want to thank Dr. Peter Baker, Lois Baker, and Stefania Lesko for their love and support. And to my wife, Deborah Lesko Baker, go all my thanks and gratitude for a gift that overwhelms the understanding.

Introduction

The major shift in theoretical discourse of the past thirty years—especially in France—is most often seen as a "linguistic turn," incorporating the insights of linguistics as a discipline into the discourse of the human sciences.[1] Rather than seeing "man" as the organizing principle of the knowledge-centered discourses, this shift would urge that we look at language as the enabling condition for these discourses, and thus for anything that would pass for knowledge about human existence, reality, thinking, and so forth. For a relatively brief moment some theorists, who came to be called structuralists, may have even held open the possibility of a totalizing, scientific understanding of the most diverse fields, by utilizing this linguistic commonality as an organizing system. What is clear now is that even many of those who were called structuralists did not hold to any such belief and were in fact even at the time producing writings to challenge such an ideal. So whereas the structuralists had an organizing principle, even if short-lived and impossible to attain and with perhaps no adherents, those thinkers to whom we refer as poststructuralists seem to have even less of a common program or system of ideas. I want to argue here that some of these theorists, notably Jacques Derrida, Jacques Lacan, Emmanuel Levinas, Julia Kristeva, and Michel Foucault, do in fact share concerns and allied forms of questioning those concerns. In the breach opened up by placing into question, or the deconstruction, if you will, of the traditional or humanist subject as a rational, willing agent, these thinkers in various ways have all been engaged to some extent in exploring what I will here be calling the ethical subject of discourse.

One problem with referring to a shared or allied project centered on ethics for such a variety of theoretical positions is that each of them explicitly rejects the ethical thinking tied to the tradition of the rational, judging or thetic subject. In this, as many others have commented before me, these French thinkers are taking seriously Friedrich Nietzsche's description of the traditional thinking on ethics as reflecting clearly and directly the justification for their position of eminence by a powerful elite.[2] Not only does the elite guard its position of power and domination through recourse to ethical justification, but those in the position of the powerless and dispossessed are handed a ready-made moral code (corresponding in its prescriptive function to the ethical justification of the elite) which compensates them for their suffering while reinforcing the conditions that enable this suffering to continue. Nietzsche's own recourse, in response to this condition of domination and the enslavement of thinking, was to the "will to power" and "eternal return," as is relatively well known (as well as beyond the scope of my current inquiry). What some critics have attempted recently is to show the derivation of the thinking of the poststructuralists from this Nietzschean model. Jürgen Habermas, for example, argues in *The Philosophical Discourse of Modernity* that Derrida and Foucault follow two diverging branches or movements out of Nietzsche's thought: Derrida's based on Nietzsche's nihilism or critique of presence, and Foucault's based on the critique of power relations as they determine the position of the individual subject.[3] Habermas presents this argument in an attempt to show how both of these lines of thinking eventually lead to dead-end positions, which in turn demonstrates that Nietzsche took a wrong turn from the enlightenment thinking of Kant, Hegel, and Marx. Habermas argues against what he sees as the irrationalist and nihilist positions of Nietzsche, urging a recovery of the enlightenment subject for the present-day purposes of social critique, based on his model of communicative reason. I return to my reasons for disagreeing with Habermas's overall position in the next chapter, in relation to the writings of Christopher Norris, but for the moment I want to explore Habermas's tracing of the Nietzschean lineage in both Derrida and Foucault.

It seems crucial to me to acknowledge that both Derrida and Foucault follow Nietzsche in rejecting the possibility of a normative ethics based on a universal human subject.[4] We might even agree heuristically with Habermas and say that Derrida does this through a critique of the presence of the self to itself, and Foucault through a critique of the power relations that determine the social constitution of the self.

We also must note, however, that Derrida's critique of the self-presence of the self is related to questions of power and violence, and Foucault's view of power relations undermines the self-consistency of the self. I would argue further that both Derrida and Foucault, as different as their works would appear to be, are engaged in this Nietzschean critique at roughly the same time as the so-called structuralist movement is the most prominent, that is to say, the late sixties. When Foucault pronounces *"la fin de l'homme"* (the end of man) in *Les mots et les choses* (1966) or when Derrida proclaims that *"il n'y a pas de hors-texte"* (there is no outside-the-text) in *De la grammatologie* (1967), neither is pledging allegiance to structuralism. The "science of signs" that both in some sense proclaim removes once and for all the reified image of the human subject, as well as invalidating all recourse to a quasi-substantial human nature, in the study of language as well as social relations. The challenge that both theorists set out—and, I would say, their hidden gift—is how to reimagine or redescribe intersubjective relations in the wake of this radical striking out of the enlightenment image of man as the source for our descriptions of both who we are and what is. One could say that, for each, *alterity* emerges as the sign of intersubjective relations and the *ethical subject of discourse* as its necessary corollary.

The primarily chronological order in this book of these movements has as one goal to place these theories of the subject in the context of phenomenological currents. The third chapter investigates the phenomenology of Maurice Merleau-Ponty, whose death in 1961 cut short a promising and tantalizing direction for thinking the constitution of the subject in relation to the body and world. Gilles Deleuze, in his relatively recent book *Foucault* (1986), devotes a surprising amount of discussion to the similarities between Foucault's discussion of the body and that of Merleau-Ponty (117ff.). Lacan's discussion of Merleau-Ponty's philosophy, which provides the primary focus, outlines three important areas of Merleau-Ponty's thinking: the relation of the subject to the perceived world, the relation of the subject to others, and the self-constitution of the subject. But then he says that his only interest is in the final problem, with the first two areas entering into his discussion only as they affect the third. This, of course, prepares the way for Lacan to investigate, in a "fundamental" way, his theory of the misrecognition of the subject in its own desire. The important point, in terms of this introductory contextualizing of different approaches, is the general resonance of Lacan's theory of the split subject with Foucault's and Derrida's rejection of the reason-centered subject of the enlightenment, leaving aside any argument for Lacan as a typically postmodern figure. Thus, Lacan's relation to Merleau-Ponty's thinking is exemplary of the historical break between poststructuralism and phenomenology, a break that at the same time acknowledges the continuity and continuing resource of the earlier philosophical movement, an acknowledgement often missing in other poststructuralist texts.

Phenomenology also provides a background for the emergence of difference as the topic of the third chapter, with the overall focus on how this concept, or the related nonconcept of *différance,* emerges in the late thinking of Heidegger, is then theorized in a post-Kantian manner by Gilles Deleuze, and is eventually radicalized in the early works of Derrida. In the philosophy of Heidegger the repeated question around which his thinking organizes itself is the ontological difference, or the difference between Being and beings, sometimes phrased as a question: Why should there be Being instead of nothing at all? In contrast to some current-day interpreters of Derrida, I believe that it is imperative to heed the repeated assertions in Derrida's own writings that his thinking develops an area opened up by the Heideggerian questioning. If the seriousness of Derrida's philosophical project is to be maintained, and its full impact, weight, and scope recognized, there is simply no way to sidestep his involvement with Heidegger. The development of difference in Derrida's early works shows an interesting contrast with the work from the same time frame by Gilles Deleuze. In his work on repetition Deleuze displays both philosophical rigor and some of the potential problems for a theoretical language that remains in some sense within the post-Kantian paradigm. Thus the radicality of Derrida's *différance* emerges: both the rootedness of his discourse in the Heideggerian questioning and the break in the language itself for describing the problematic when compared with that of Deleuze.

Let there be no doubt then that Derrida emerges as the protagonist of this literary-theoretical narrative. Derrida's radical thought on *différance* and the enlarged sense of "writing" he urges in the *Grammatology* emerge as much more than a theory of textual practice or reading or hermeneutics. When Derrida says in the *Grammatology* that "writing" in the large sense he gives it can only be thought within the "horizon of intersubjective violence" (G 185; trans. 127), he *shatters,* in a way that has still to be adequately thought through and recognized, the complacency of any view that rests within the confines of the academy or is only concerned with the act of reading and interpreting texts. His misunderstood pronouncement that "there is nothing outside the text" means, from this perspective, that all intersubjective forms of violence, domination and exploitation need to be analyzed as forms of "writing," where writing stands obviously for much more than words on a page.[5] As with the writings of Foucault that are much more commonly interpreted in this way, Derrida's writings call for deconstruction as a form of resistance to intersubjective violence. Can violence ever be successfully and completely resisted, even in the work of deconstruction? Such is the question around which much of his later work turns, and such is the question of the ethical subject of discourse.

Emmanuel Levinas has raised this question of the ethical subject, especially in relation to the other, and to the call of the other that Levinas terms *exteriority*. Levinas's work provides a crucial locus for exploring a subject positioning based on such an exteriority. Derrida's own writing bears a complex relationship to that of Levinas, as others have shown (and which the last chapter further explores). My previous work on poetic theory and interpretation, *Obdurate Brilliance: Exteriority and the Modern Long Poem*, expanded on and adapted Levinas's theory of exteriority as a model of text production and interpretation. The primary focus in this study is rather Levinas's principal works in their philosophical and religious contexts, as well as in the context of other poststructuralist writers such as Derrida, Maurice Blanchot, Jean-François Lyotard, and Luce Irigaray. In my view, Levinas's writing on exteriority sets out a direction that parallels the resistance to intersubjective violence that Derrida calls for in the *Grammatology*. This chapter also develops a critical discussion of Derrida's early essay, almost an "attack" on Levinas, "Violence and Metaphysics." My view is that Derrida's work has in fact changed and evolved over the past thirty years, becoming closer in its ethical stance to that of Levinas. Levinas's work has its controversial aspects as well, as when he expresses his view of woman as essentially *other*. This nodal point of Levinas's thought attracts the attention of Luce Irigaray, as well as Derrida, and continues to raise questions for the discourses of theoretical feminism, questions that indicate the important place of feminism in postmodern theory.

The focus on women in relation to the ethical subject of discourse leads to a discussion of Julia Kristeva's "ethical feminism." This argument is based on a view of Kristeva as operating out of the Lacanian breach in the subject opened by the misrecognition of the subject in its own desire. Kristeva's famous distinction of signifying functions between the symbolic and the semiotic thus can be seen to further the Lacanian topos of the Symbolic, the Imaginary, and the Real, by extending attention to how the Imaginary expresses itself in the semiotic disposition of the text.[6] Kristeva, while maintaining a clearly defined distance from the feminist movements in France, develops her psychoanalytic insights into the ethical subject of discourse in part by working with models of mother-child identification in ways that Lacan's male-centered discourse would not allow.[7] Kristeva's apparently paradoxical distance from French feminism can be seen as her response to the normative position of traditional ethics discussed earlier. Kristeva's theories, like those of Foucault and Derrida, are clearly based, at least in part, on a Nietzschean distrust of any ethics that posits set norms for personal and social behavior. From Kristeva's depth psychoanalytical perspective, normative ethics are another name for the repressive *Nom du père* of the Lacanian Symbolic realm. Her work with pre-Oedipal— and thus pre-Symbolic—structures of mother-child identification lead to her challenging theories of abjection and depression; this, in turn, is of special interest to women, but *not* in the terms of the normative social-symbolic code, whether of the patriarchy or what Kristeva views as "official" (what I term "normative") feminism. This chapter also presents an investigation of Kristeva's work with respect to artistic production, applied specifically to a reading of a film, *The Silence of the Lambs*. This is obviously a test of the applicability of Kristeva's theories; but it also serves to reinforce a contrast between the power and insight generated by her theories, and the normative sociosymbolic interpretive structures that Wayne Booth calls ethical criticism, and the empty deconstructive gestures that Hillis Miller claims as an ethics of reading.

The final chapters return to the work of Jacques Derrida, particularly that work which his proponents who want to insist on his seriousness and his philosophical rigor tend to avoid. Chapter 6 examines the question of the "impossibility" of deconstruction. The discussion is linked to the earlier treatment of Derrida in the chapter on difference through a more thorough examination of the functioning of the *reste*, or remainder, in *Glas* (1974). Although this work is treated in the English-language criticism almost solely as an exercise in "free-play" and textual experimentalism, I return again to Derrida's contrast between the totalizing ethical system proposed by Hegel's *Philosophy of Right* and the unassimilable remainder forever outside the philosopher's system that Derrida finds exemplified in *le cas Genet* (the case of Genet). Gay and lesbian theorists have been energized particularly in response to Foucault's work on the social constitution of sex and gender identity; yet Genet's work, especially in the light of Derrida's discussion of it in *Glas*, likewise represents the unassimilable *other*, both "Out" and therefore in some sense radically "Inside" the sociosymbolic constitution of gender identity.[8] Identity, as it is constituted by practices of text and self, is elusive, and thus finally escapes Hegel's logic, his normative ethics of the family, gender roles, and capital punishment as the founding societal instance. The contrast between Hegel and Genet leads to questioning what is *proper* about the proper name, whether the familial metaphors Hegel employs are also a way of drawing boundaries around the philosophical project.

Derrida's more recent texts continue to work around these theoretical boundaries by invoking terms such as *différance, le reste, restance, parergon,* and so on, as well as to expand the range of his references and his texts for analysis. Derrida has also continued to interrogate what is proper in the proper name, raising questions about his own implication in the process of writing through a kind of "negative" autobiography (the subject of chapter 7).[9] His textual practice has moved in the direction of exploring what the parameters are for ethical discourse and specifically the practice of an ethical deconstruction. One limit these texts approach is simply the limit of understanding, posing the question of whether deconstruction as ethical practice is even possible. But in posing this question of the "impossible" ethics of deconstruction, what emerges, in contrast to normative ethical standards based on a set of rules or injunctions, is an other-directed discourse that is patient, open-ended, and responsive to the highest ethical demand. Derrida continues to investigate the Heideggerian area of questioning, which includes facing the most difficult questions concerning Heidegger's involvement with Nazism. These questions are coimplicated with the direction and movements of Western thought as a whole that have given rise to Nazism and other movements of totalizing, systematic control of thought and populations. Conceivably as part of his autobiographical project, Derrida has contributed searching responses to the fact of the Holocaust, and its continuing presence/absence in memory and flame and ashes. He has also continued to engage in dialogue with the work of Levinas in ways that border on collage, impersonation, and cross-quotation. And he has interrogated the question of whether or not deconstruction shares features with negative theology and thinking about the apocalypse. In all these ways, the "impossible" ethics of deconstruction continue to seek forms for resistance to inter-subjective violence. Through pursuing an autobiographical writing, Derrida draws attention to "impossibility" as an aspect of singularity in written texts. He thus insists on the ethical character of deconstructive inquiry as a question of critical responsibility, while at the same time attempting to situate his texts in a nonuniversalizing, nonnormative context.

The chapter immediately following this introduction represents an attempt to bring a focus to what I am calling the ethical subject of discourse—issues of language, ethics, and critical responsibility, particularly with respect to the theories of Derrida—by examining recent work on deconstruction by two prominent Anglophone critics, Robert Scholes and Christopher Norris. I also address the issue of the centrality given to Derrida's thinking by looking at some alternative formulations in the work of Michel Foucault. The humanist subject, present to itself as the locus of judgment and value, seems to be a sturdier construct in English-language discourse than in the French. Those early salvos by Foucault and Derrida may have reached an attentive audience in France; but in the United States there remains a tendency to view their most radical statements as temporary aberrations.[10] My specific focus here on the recent work of Robert Scholes, which presents itself as an effort of appropriation and domestication for American audiences of the French theoretical project, provides a way of examining the issue of critical appropriation. By training close attention on key moments in Scholes's discussion of Derrida, I aim to defend Derrida's project from the limiting and mistaken (I believe) label of "nihilist hermeneutics" that Scholes proposes in *Protocols of Reading*. In particular, Scholes's reading remains persistently blind to the social and real-world significance of Derrida's project, especially as Scholes ignores the constitutive role of intersubjective violence in Derrida's philosophy. By appropriating and taming Derrida's deconstruction to "protocols of reading," Scholes both limits and misreads Derrida's project. There is also the question of the pragmatic consequences of such a reading, that is, whether Scholes really means to ally himself, as such a reading must inevitably do, with those critics who seek to defuse the force of deconstruction by repeating commonly held misconceptions about Derrida's work, thus resisting or refusing to recognize its real-world effects.[11]

Since the proper names Derrida and Foucault have been linked throughout this introductory presentation, there remains another question to be asked: Why not Foucault? If Foucault's project of demonstrating the power relations within which subjects constitute themselves shares features with Derridean deconstruction, why follow out the one direction and not the other? One possible answer has to do with the kind of pragmatic question raised with relation to the work of Scholes. What are the consequences of presenting the constitution of the subject as resulting from practices of knowledge that are also and always techniques of power? Is there some justification in the repeated charges that Foucault creates a subjectless universe of implacable discursive forces? Was he the only one to recognize this and did he thus create for himself a position somehow "outside" the totalizing system he claimed to be describing, a position which therefore can only be occupied by himself? Did he, in his focus on sexuality and the ethics of care for the self, limit his later writings in a way which, while useful to some, likewise writes out many others? By addressing some of these questions, I mean to situate the decision to focus on Derrida rather than Foucault, as well as to face some of the necessary limitations in my own discursive position.

The intricate trajectory that Christopher Norris traces in his recent work provides additional material to clarify these issues and to establish what my position will be in this book. Norris's overall stated goal in *What's Wrong with Postmodernism* (1990) is to maintain a real-world efficacy for deconstructive actions. As much as I value Norris's attempt to bring Derridean deconstruction into a usable conjunction with Frankfurt school critical theory, his efforts to do so require him to make some very suspect moves. Habermas's theory of communicative reason cannot be allied with Derrida's project of deconstruction without giving rise to some serious, even debilitating, misunderstandings. These same misunderstandings would also seem to underlie Norris's attempt to dissociate Derrida from the thinking of Heidegger. Norris's strange denial of the Heidegger-Derrida connection is intricately related to his attempt to recuperate Paul de Man's later writings as pointing to deconstruction's real-world effects, but here too there are serious gaps when it comes to proving his case. And yet Norris's push to demonstrate the political and real-world efficacy of deconstruction remains of value and, in turn, adumbrates many of the issues raised later in this book.

In the following chapters, I return to the chronological ordering, in part to offer one possible narrative concerning the rise of deconstructive and other theories of the ethical subject. The view of the ethical subject of discourse that emerges in the work of Derrida, Foucault, and others, I will be claiming, relates in complex—and not always openly avowed—ways to the French tradition of phenomenology. Jacques Lacan's reading of Merleau-Ponty's later philosophy is paradigmatic of both this indebtedness—which he openly avows—as well as the shift in emphasis to the self-constitution of the subject in language. The discussion of Gilles Deleuze and Derrida in the context of Heidegger's thinking on difference likewise seeks to establish the thinking and practice of a certain time. Seeing how a thinker of great acuity and innovatory tendencies like Deleuze nonetheless remains restrained by a post-Kantian philosophical vocabulary makes it possible to place Derrida's radical thought in the *Grammatology* into proper perspective. The difficult, if not impossible, task is to maintain awareness of ethical thinking in deconstruction, which is a reason to examine the ethical philosophy of Levinas in the context of other theorists who link their vocabularies and approaches to his, or offer their own critiques. The rise of feminist theorizing, whether or not it is embraced as such by someone like Kristeva, operates in a determined way out of the same ethical sphere. In the final chapters, I deal with Derrida's later philosophy, first suggesting how his philosophical trajectory has led him increasingly to examine ethical issues, while insisting, often through the sheer difficulty of his texts, on just how hard this is to do. I close by looking at Derrida's idiosyncratic move into what I will be calling his "negative" autobiography as one strategy for dealing with these ethical issues in a textual practice that resists assimilation to normative philosophical models of the subject.

Chapter One

The Ethical Subject of Discourse

As part of the investigation into what I am here calling the ethical subject of discourse in deconstructive theory and other related postmodern theoretical projects, there are many decisions that obviously have to be made about how to situate one's own discourse. As a practical matter of writing in English for primarily American academic audiences, including students of critical theory, one always arrives to a certain extent after the introductions have been made. By examining the critical projects of Robert Scholes and Christopher Norris, I want to situate the issues with which this study will be dealing. Having made the choice to return repeatedly to the works of Jacques Derrida, I also want to clarify the political and discursive dimensions of such a choice by contrasting it with some of the main theories of Michel Foucault and their reception by significant American critics. In ordering the presentation as I do, I am following an itinerary that consists of first examining questions of language and reference with respect to Scholes's work; then investigating questions of discursive positioning with respect to Foucault; and, finally, questioning the ethics of criticism generally with respect to Norris's project of claiming a political and real-world dimension for deconstruction. The order of the presentation is thus not chronological but follows the logical progression of language, from the smallest units of meaning, words and reference, to discursive functioning, to the social context of criticism. This focus on key issues within a context of Anglo-American criticism in turn will help to prefigure elements of the discussion when dealing primarily with French theorists in the subsequent chapters.

Scholes Unfair to Derrida?

Robert Scholes apparently believes that the arguments he presents in *Protocols of Reading* effectively refute Derrida's theory of "writing" in the larger sense to which I have been alluding, but do they really, and is Scholes really fair in his overall strategies? Briefly stated, Derrida demonstrates in the *Grammatology* that the written mark is always inhabited by the workings of the *trace*, in that the mark is always working to differentiate itself from its previous meaning in such a way as to effect a time delay between that previous meaning and its current one. Part of Derrida's strategy is to show that the trace, and thus the workings of *différance* (which I examine in detail in chapter 3), operates in any kind of sign, whether written or spoken, thus reversing the traditional priority assigned to speech over writing. Scholes, however, argues that "presence" is inescapable in two linguistic functions: deixis and the first-person pronoun. Since presence is necessarily implicated in these two workings of *spoken* language, according to Scholes, Derrida is wrong about the relationship of writing to speech and can only be called "nihilist" if he continues to deny such active linguistic presence.

For arguments as potentially important as these, Scholes's supporting evidence is remarkably slim. Arguing in favor of the presence of the referent in the deixis of the speech act, Scholes states: "One of those crucial differences is that we all learn the first elements of language through communication with another person in the presence of objects that can be named. I am forcibly reminded of this when my neighbor Brad, who is approaching his third birthday, comes over for a visit. Much of his speech takes the form of 'What's that?' with the aid of a pointing finger" (71). So plain and commonsensical, so self-evident, is this little story, that Scholes goes on to proclaim: "I cannot imagine that Derrida wants to deny that we learn language in this way" (71). Scholes's imaginative difficulty masks a pseudo-naive stance here, since not only Derrida, but many theorists of the postmodern subject, including Wittgenstein and Foucault, would not only deny this version of how one acquires language, but have devoted considerable book-length works to doing so. Wittgenstein begins his *Philosophical Investigations* with almost exactly the same anecdote, taken from Saint Augustine's *Confessions*. This theory of language is especially important to Wittgenstein, since he held to a version of it in his *Tractatus* and tried to work out systematically its results for a fully logical philosophy. This in turn allied him closely at the time with Bertrand Russell, to whom Scholes refers for support (*Protocols* 71–73). Wittgenstein's turn to what now gets called his later philosophy was provoked by his rejection of this language of logical simples. One could argue, *grosso modo*, that the whole of the *Philosophical Investigations* constitutes a critique of the Augustinian/Scholesian theory of language. Again, simplifying greatly, one could say further that Wittgenstein comes up with language games as a core concept around which his refutation of Augustine revolves. Thus we could say, following Wittgenstein, that Scholes's neighbor Brad is already quite adept at this particular language game that involves pointing to an object and saying "What's that?" Brad's obvious skill in playing this game indicates from the perspective of Wittgenstein's theory of language (and current psycholinguistics generally) that Brad already has a good working knowledge of what constitutes language games in general.[1] One might even guess that Scholes's scarcely concealed pleasure in participating in this particular game could well be what Brad is responding to in the first place.

Foucault's argument in *Les mots et les choses* is that the Augustinian/ Scholesian model of language is one with a particular historical framework, participating in the preclassical *episteme* in which the sign was the logical and unproblematic correlative of the thing, its natural symbol. In the classical episteme the whole question of representation becomes a question for theory, and grammarians work out the ratios in a way which defines in some sense the world view of the eighteenth century. The shift to the modern episteme is provoked by the breakdown of the classical ratios of relation between the thing and the sign. In the modern episteme the level of relation of these two is one that Foucault (and following him, Deleuze) characterizes as one of "non-rapport" (see Deleuze, *Foucault* 68ff.). Since signs and things, or the sayable and the representable, constitute two separate layers of experience and reality, the thinking subject *à la* Descartes gets invented in order to synthesize the two layers at the level of the interiorized thought of the subject. *Les mots et les choses*, with its *"fin de l'homme,"* announces the end of the modern episteme—and ushers in the postmodern—by questioning the interiorizing subject or "I" as in the modern *cogito*.

Scholes wants to hold on to the interiorizing subject or "I," at least in the instance of the person speaking who says "I," who must be "present" in Scholes's view for the utterance to occur, at least from the practical, empiricist standpoint. Scholes, oddly, invokes Émile Benveniste's characterization of the "I" as a *shifter* in order to prove the existence of the person speaking in the individual speech act. I say it is odd because once again virtually every contemporary language theorist has used Benveniste's construct to answer the tricky question of whether the utterance must have an ontological relation with the person who speaks it. Again, this is one of the main issues that Foucault raises in *Les mots et les choses*. In order to believe in the presence of the person speaking the utterance, we need a cultural concept of the person, or *man*. As Foucault says, famously: "Western culture has constructed, under the name of man, a being which by one and the same play of reasoning, must be a positive domain of *knowledge* and cannot be an object of *science*."[2] In other words, according to Foucault, the modern episteme is constructed around the rational subject who knows as opposed to being an object for study. Wittgenstein goes after the person who self-knowingly says "I" in the elocutory instance in *The Blue and Brown Books*. He claims that it is the continuity of bodily existence, the resemblance of one's body to itself over time, that gives an individual a false sense of identity and thus masks the lack of identity in the elocutory instance.[3] Of course, one element of Derrida's whole project has been to show that utterances have meaning, effects, and a certain kind of existence, in the absence of the speaker, receiver, or referent. In "Signature, Event, Context," for example, he works out the reasons why the possible absence of the enunciating subject is a founding condition of the utterance coming about and attaining the status of an utterance at all.

Scholes's attempted refutation of Derrida's work on "writing" virtually ignores the dimension of intersubjective violence that Derrida has investigated in relation to the use of the proper name. Derrida's devastating critique in the *Grammatology* of Lévi-Strauss's famous "writing lesson" targets the anthropologist's claim that the Nambikwara lack writing, by saying: "If writing is no longer understood in the narrow sense of linear and phonetic notation, it should be possible to say that all societies capable of producing, that is to say obliterating, their proper names, and of bringing classificatory difference into play, practice writing in general" (G 161; trans. 109). A less obvious, yet no less serious, investigation by Derrida into this problematic of the proper name is that of *le cas Genet* (the case of Genet) presented in *Glas*. Brad in Scholes's narrative is merely paying a visit to his neighbor; we are meant to assume that Brad has both a mother and father who love him and care for him and, among other things, teach him the names of the objects to which he points. Derrida's discussion of Hegel in *Glas* shows among other things how all sorts of unexamined familial metaphors enter into the support for Hegel's universal system. But what happens to the child who is abandoned, as Genet was? What is there "proper" about his proper name? Is his childhood experience any less universal than Brad's? Or does the *cas Genet* serve rather as a warning against the kind of universal philosophical project that Hegel engaged in and to which Scholes continues, in his way, to pledge allegiance? Derrida draws his example of Genet's early life from Genet's own writings, whereas Scholes apparently has selected Brad from his own direct experience, but it actually doesn't make the least bit of difference to the story presented in *Protocols of Reading* whether "Brad" is the child's real name, whether such a child exists, or whether, if so, he ever said or did any of the things Scholes claims he did. In other words, little "Brad" has, strictly speaking, the same ontological status—that is, an *exemplum* in a written text—as little "Jean" in Genet's texts and Derrida's texts about Genet, and little "Jean" to me is much more real and says more about my ethical responsibility as a thinking and writing subject.

This is the fundamental problem with the label Scholes assigns to Derrida's project of "nihilist hermeneutics." The only thing *nihilist* means in this context is that Scholes is interpreting Derrida's work within a certain framework that has for founding conceptual grounds some deeply held beliefs in presence and the actual self-presence of speaking beings. Outside of this framework, which is where Derrida clearly sees himself as operating and as much as anything else is what Scholes disputes, the term *nihilist* means strictly nothing.[4] Scholes is simply mistaken to argue that Derrida wants to claim that little "Brad" doesn't exist, or for that matter that little "Jean" doesn't exist. What Derrida argues is that the structure of writing in the general sense guarantees that we can make no neat distinctions between "Brad"'s ontological status and that of "Jean." Whether Genet invented his own identity in his books is a significant line of inquiry, but not one that can be solved simply by recourse to certain kinds of documentation.[5] In fact, from my point of view, Derrida's philosophy, far from being nihilist, gives much more direct access to the very real areas of experience that Scholes's empiricism causes him to elide. Such areas of experience are, for example, those of class, race, gender, and sexuality. Scholes leaves out of his presentation all analysis of (but, very significantly, *not* all reference to) his own interpellation in systems of wealth, power, privilege, and status—and then he asks us to accept his and "Brad"'s experience as both universal and true. And it is on the basis of the truth of his experience that Scholes asks us to reject Derrida's work as nihilist; when in fact one significant thing Derrida's work on "writing" does is make more visible our participation in such systems of wealth, power, and privilege. These ethicopolitical systems, in turn, determine in advance and in a nontrivial sense what we can do, say, or write.

Derrida's project, in Scholes's view, is both nihilist in its rejection of real experience and limited to methods of reading texts, and thus merely a hermeneutics. This latter claim is also unnecessarily limiting and ultimately mistaken. Because Scholes can only see Derrida's statement of *"il n'y a pas de hors-texte"* as saying that we can only interpret written documents, he claims that deconstruction is limited to a practice of reading these documents. Since this misreading is so widespread, Derrida has many times tried to correct it, as when he says, for example: "I never cease to be surprised by critics who see my work as a declaration that there is nothing beyond language, that we are imprisoned in language; it is, in fact, saying the exact opposite. The critique of logocentrism is above all else the search for the 'other' and the 'other of language'" ("Deconstruction and the Other" 123). Derrida says elsewhere: "when it is said about the deconstructive perspective that there is nothing outside the text, then I say to myself: If deconstruction *really* consisted in saying that everything happens in books, it wouldn't deserve *five* minutes of anybody's attention" ("Deconstruction in America" 15; italics in original).[6] Scholes must be aware at some level of these various statements made by Derrida. What can his stake be in claiming that deconstruction is only a matter of reading texts, unless it is to present his own version of a textual practice that is "really" connected to the outside world?

Scholes presents his own paradigm for reading in the form of a discussion of a painting, *The Education of the Virgin*, that is variously attributed to Georges de la Tour or one of his followers and that we find reprinted on the cover of *Protocols of Reading*. Like the brief narrative concerning "Brad," this pictorial image could be characterized either as sweet or as dangerously complacent. As with his discussion of Derrida's theory of writing in general, what gets left out in Scholes's reading is what Derrida calls "the violence of the letter." What happens to Scholes's paradigm of reading if the exemplary pictorial text is not *The Education of the Virgin*, but rather an image like Titian's *The Flaying of Marsyas* (Titian catalogue 370–72)? Like Scholes's example, Titian's painting is also of doubtful attribution, and critics are divided as to its meaning. In the painting, the satyr Marsyas is being skinned alive while hanging upside down. Marsyas, as may be recalled, had the misfortune to lose a musical contest with Apollo. The wager between them was that the winner could do what he liked with the loser. What divides the critics of Titian's painting is their interpretation of the attitudes of the other figures in the painting, who seem curiously contemplative in the face of the horrifying event depicted. Clearly, however, some complex of attitudes toward *aesthesis* is involved, taking into account this word's etymological root of physical sensation. Marsyas's very real suffering (or is it? how would we judge this?) is the object of the surrounding figures' indifference or thoughtful contemplation, but music and merrymaking continue, reminding the viewer of the artistic contest as well perhaps as the viewers' aesthetic enjoyment of the scene.[7] Scholes's elision of the violent underpinnings of any discursive situation does violence to Derrida's text and dissimulates this violence in the guise of a copacetic conversation with books and friends.[8]

Why Not Foucault?

As much as any one concern in Michel Foucault's writing, what dominates his writings over his whole career is the problematic of the identity of the self, at least early on in his humanist or enlightenment model of the disinterested intellectual as writer of texts. My whole discussion of Scholes's author-position in *Protocols of Reading* could probably be aptly summarized in a one-or-two sentence Foucauldian description of the "universal intellectual" (Foucault, *Foucault Reader*, 67ff.). The position that Derrida establishes through his riffs on the signature of the author could likewise be compared with Foucault's investigation, "What Is an Author?" And yet one lingering question about Foucault's work is the extent to which he sees himself as escaping the networks of power relations that determine what one can do or say and what counts as a true utterance.[9] How valid is the critique of Foucault's position that focuses on the way Foucault extricates himself from the totalizing discursive systems he subjects to analysis?

The recent discussion of Foucault's career has tended to avoid this question, or at least to blunt it, through a periodization of his work. If Foucault did hold to a position for himself that was "outside" the discursive network of power relations, some have claimed that this was a short-lived period of his writing which he redeemed in his later work that focuses precisely on the constitution of the individual self, by implication his own included. Mark Poster, for example, views the three periods of Foucault's production very schematically: the first was the work during the sixties and the dismantling of the Cartesian self; the second was Foucault's work in the 1970s and the shift "from subject to structure;" and the third, his last work, "(which Foucault was to call ethics), was a hermeneutics of the self using a strategy of *historicism:* [when] the emphasis fell to the self-constitution in discursive practices" (54). This schema is altogether too neat, in that it claims historicism as the reigning paradigm for only the final period, when clearly historicism was at issue from the beginning. One could rightly question whether the "hermeneutics of the self," which does seem apt to describe Foucault's final work, really constitutes a historicism at all, in the sense that his earlier work clearly did. What is needed is a return to the period of the *fin de l'homme,* to examine the austerity of Foucault's project in giving the subject of enlightenment rationality its most radical critique, corresponding in its way to Derrida's critique of presence.

The model for the human sciences, in the French appellation, invoked in the previous introduction, should have also served as a clear invocation of Foucault's model for analyzing the appearance of the concept of "man." In *Les mots et les choses,* for example, Foucault states: "the naked fact that . . . man, alone or with others, should have become the object of science—this cannot be considered or treated as a phenomenon of belief: it is an event in the order of knowledge."[10] But just as the concept of "man" constructs itself as the basis for any kind of knowledge concerning biology, economics, or language (Foucault's three areas of inquiry), so a shift in the episteme can just as certainly constitute the end of "man" in this foundational or regulative sense. And this is what has happened in our era, according to Foucault, in a shift that was first announced by Nietzsche and that has only with the work of Foucault and others become subject to perspicuous analysis. This, for Foucault, is the meaning of the eternal return of Nietzsche's philosophy: "If the discovery of the Return is really the end of philosophy, the *end of man* is itself the return of the beginning of philosophy. In our time one can no longer think except in the empty space of man's disappearance. Because this emptiness is not a lack, it does not prescribe a gap to fill. It is nothing more, nothing less, than the unfolding of a space where it is finally possible once again to think."[11] This well-known aspect of Foucault's thinking shows a similar thrust to that which can also be found, as is less well-known, in Derrida's thinking in the *Grammatology*. From the point of view of the archaeologist Foucault, the erasure of the concept of man allows for a new scientific approach to questions that had been obscured by the concept of the humanist subject. In Derrida's thinking, the self-presence of the self to itself in the act of speech is a similar myth, one that obscures the workings of the linguistic sign and leads to chimeras such as thought as a form of interiorized silent speech and the speaker's presumed intentionality.

I have found in pursuing my investigations of *exteriority* that this idea of the interior self as the founding reality for human individuals is something virtually everyone I know wants to hold on to. We (they and I) might see as an acceptable metaphor for a shift in the episteme the famous image at the end of *Les mots et les choses* in which "man" is seen as being as ephemeral as a mark left in the sand which the oncoming tide is about to erase, but no one I know—with the exception of my Buddhist friends—is ready to accept that the inner self is not the locus for value and truth, the guarantor of experience. But the disappearance of "man" means just that.[12] As Foucault says in a 1967 interview about *Les mots et les choses*, "Thus the contemporary critic is abandoning the great myth of interiority: *intimior intimio ejus*. He finds himself totally displaced from the old themes of locked enclosures, of the treasure in the box that he habitually sought in the depth of the work's container. Placing himself at the exterior of the text, he constitutes a new exterior for it, writing texts out of texts" (*Foucault Live* 21). The threat of exteriority, that the self is not present to itself in a transparent way, not even in the moment of utterance, is as much as anything what a critic like Scholes can be shown to be reacting against. If there is no interiority, in his view, there can be no locus, no place in which to reconcile the nonlinguistic experience of waves and sunlight with the linguistic experience of texts. What Foucault and Derrida share is the effort of thinking required to escape that interiorizing "box" where these experiences of different levels are seen to come together in our cultural view of ourselves, and that in turn serves as a basis for our thinking about anything else. But Foucault is no more a nihilist than Derrida, as some would claim (see Dreyfus and Rabinow, 86–87). Waves and sunlight (examples used by Scholes) are real experiences, I would say, but the idea that they come to have meaning in some kind of interior space that constitutes the thinking subject is no more nor less than a cultural construct. Given the persistence of the interiority myth, one understands why Nietzsche felt the need to philosophize with a hammer.

Philosophizing with a hammer seems a mighty violent response when compared with the simple experience of sunlight and waves, but then Foucault's subsequent work is designed to show that the epistemology of the self in the work of cultural constructs is a violent process. This violent process is the power/knowledge relation that Foucault works out in such texts as *La volonté de savoir* (*History of Sexuality* 1). The interior space of the individual subject comes into being through the actions of power relations: "Between technologies of knowledge and strategies of power, no exteriority, even if each has its own specific role and each articulates itself by means of the other, *starting from their differences.*"[13] In a line of thinking that will prove decisive for the subsequent theorists of gender and sexual identity, Foucault states very clearly the relation between the progression of epistemological change and the individual human subject: "The body is the inscribed surface of events (traced by language and dissolved by ideas), the locus of a dissociated self (adopting the illusion of a substantial unity), and a volume in perpetual disintegration. Genealogy, as an analysis of descent, is thus situated within the articulation of the body and history. Its task is to expose a body totally imprinted by history and the process of history's destruction of the body" (NGH 148). Sexuality is thus not an arbitrary choice for Foucault's genealogical researches. (I return to this question in examining Foucault's later works.) As the panoptical model of *Surveiller et punir* (*Discipline and Punish*) indicates the knowledge-aspect of social control, so the body as the place of inscription of power relations necessarily implicates sexuality. The progress of knowledge is thus not linked to liberation in Foucault's view; rather, as he says, "Humanity installs each of its violences in a system of rules and thus proceeds from domination to domination" (NGH 151). As Deleuze notes, violence is a concomitant element of force in Foucault's system; but in what I take to be a distinct difference from Derrida's thinking on the issue, violence is not a constituting element of force (Deleuze, *Foucault* 77).[14]

The criticism of Foucault that came to dominate discussion of his work at this time was that his philosophy proposed the raw exercise of power as an implacable, subjectless and faceless process. So we find Hubert Dreyfus and Paul Rabinow, for example, disputing this contention: "Foucault at times sounds . . . as if his intention was to situate all science as a mere product of power. This is false. Instead his goal has consistently been to isolate the interconnections of knowledge and power" (177). As for the charge that Foucault constructs for himself a privileged position outside of this system which he is the only one to be able to analyze, Dreyfus and Rabinow answer, "Foucault is not claiming to be outside of these practices of power; at the same time he is not identical to them" (203). Foucault, in his afterword to Dreyfus and Rabinow's study, faces these same questions and redirects them by focusing on the question of the subject. He will say, for example, "Thus it is not power, but the subject, which is the general theme of my research" (209). In this way, Foucault in the final phase of his work insists in some sense on the continuity with his early work, such as in *Les mots et les choses.* He also, in this afterword, outlines the ethical subject of discourse in a way that will continue to be of interest to the subsequent critics of his work, by focusing on the question of freedom. Foucault says: "When one defines the exercise of power as a mode of action upon the actions of others, when one characterizes these actions by the government of men by other men—in the broadest sense of the term [government]—one includes an important element: freedom. Power is exercised only over free subjects, and only insofar as they are free. . . . In this game freedom may well appear as the condition for the exercise of power" ("Afterword" 221). It is this theme of freedom that critics such as Charles E. Scott and John Rajchman have focused on in their inquiries about Foucault's ethics of the subject.

Foucault's project—and on this point both Scott and Rajchman are very clear—is not one of liberation. As Scott says, "The question of ethics rather than an ethics of liberation is characteristic of his discourse" (53). In Foucault's later thought, centering on the question of sexuality, this distinction is likewise apparent. Foucault states in an interview, "It seems to me that to use this ethical problem for the definition of practices of freedom is more important than the affirmation (and repetitious, at that) that sexuality or desire must be set free"

(ECS 114). Freedom only appears as a category of experience in the context of power relations; the corollary is also true, as when Foucault says, "If there are relations of power throughout every social field it is because there is freedom everywhere" (ECS 123). Freedom in Foucault's vocabulary thus has a very different sense from the enlightenment project of freeing the individual subject to utilize rationality to achieve his or her highest innate potential. When Foucault asks the Kantian question "What Is Enlightenment?" he gives a very un-Kantian answer in terms of the implied goal: "But if we are not to settle for the affirmation or the empty dream of freedom it seems to me that this historico-critical attitude must also be an experimental one. I mean that this work done at the limits of ourselves, must, on the one hand, open up a realm of historical inquiry and, on the other, put itself to the test of reality, of contemporary reality, both to grasp the points where change is possible and desirable, and to determine the precise form this change should take. This means that the historical ontology of ourselves must turn away from all projects that claim to be global or radical" ("What Is Enlightenment?" 46). This passage is rich in implications for the interpretation of Foucault's project. Freedom, which is obviously a crucial category in his thinking, is contrasted here with "the empty dream of freedom" of liberation philosophy. The area where the work of freedom takes place is "at the limits of ourselves" and this is clearly where the important question of sexuality demands to be asked. If Foucault's later philosophy is a historicism, as Poster has claimed, it is yet a nontotalizing historicism, a historicism rooted in contemporary reality and the pragmatics of change. Foucault rejects the modern enlightenment project, as defined, for example, by a thinker like Habermas, in rejecting "global or radical" projects.[15]

Freedom is not a universal project or possibility in Foucault's thinking. Rather freedom, as Rajchman explains, "would not lie in our essence but in our historically contingent singularity" (TE 109). This would explain why sexuality, specifically gay and lesbian sexuality, is not a factitious choice as an area of investigation for Foucault's research and thinking. Foucault's work "at the limits of ourselves" necessarily involves the work of opposing the system of domination within which alternative sexualities are caught and oppressed, limited and defined. Mark Poster criticizes Foucault's choice of sexuality as the focus of his later works, saying: "While the selection of sex as the arena of self-constitution may be justified on grounds of both historical and present-day importance, it cannot serve to rule out other topics, and it does not successfully delimit the question of self-constitution" (68). This statement is a perfect example of the critic setting up in the position of the universal judging subject, the subject position implicated by "global or radical" projects of enlightenment. By eliding the necessary contingency of his own position (in a manner not dissimilar to Scholes), Poster erases the experience of those writers for whom sexuality, especially sexual orientations marginalized by the dominant discourse, is in a sense the imposed subject that they are necessarily forced to deal with, as the unsettling use of the pronoun *they* indicates the contingent aspect of my own sexual/discursive position in this instance.

Judith Butler has taken a leading role in the effort to explore the Foucauldian dimension of gender identity from a feminist perspective.[16] She takes as a given Foucault's indication that gender identity is constructed largely through the discourse of the dominant society, but she takes this given as an occasion for asking, "What political possibilities are the consequence of a radical critique of the categories of identity?" (GT xi). Like Foucault, Butler puts forth a view of gender and sexual identity that is constituted in what Foucault would call the subject's freedom, that is, the possibilities of active resistance to dominant discursive structures. In this sense, gender is enacted through practices, rather than existing in some natural or inherent way in the individual subject. Butler states, "A political genealogy of gender ontologies, if it is successful, will deconstruct the substantive appearance of gender into its constitutive acts and locate and account for those acts within the compulsory frames set by the various forces that police the social appearance of gender" (33). While clearly operating in the area opened up by Foucault's genealogical researches, the verb *deconstruct* in this passage indicates a Derridean move as well. Of course, the compulsory frames that Butler invokes likewise refer to the groundbreaking essay by Adrienne Rich on compulsory heterosexuality and lesbian existence. But rather than invoke any kind of innate lesbian identity as that which resists the frames of dominant discursive practices, Butler clearly insists on the aspect of gender that is in some sense performed.

Just as little as Foucault does Butler see the question of gender and sexual identity as one of liberation. How do these practices, or gender performances, constitute an ethical framework? Rajchman says that "Foucault advances a new ethic: not an ethic of transgression, but the ethic of constant disengagement from constituted forms of experience. . . . It is thus an ethic for which freedom lies neither in self-discovery nor in the 'free-play' of language, but in a constant attempt at self-disengagement and self-invention" (MF 37, 38). This "self-disengagement and self-invention" takes place in what Butler terms a "*stylized repetition of acts*" (GT 140; italics in the original). In this way, what Butler urges is a politicization of gender performance, not merely a genealogical analysis, but an active and acting set of practices that deliberately challenge social norms. Butler's work in the area that Foucault suggested take place "at the limit of ourselves" rejects the notion repeatedly voiced in some feminist discourses that deconstruction and Foucauldian practice deny the identity of the subject and so necessarily block effective agency. As Butler says, "Construction is not opposed to agency; it is the necessary scene of agency, the very terms in which agency is articulated and becomes culturally intelligible" (GT 147). Just as it is crucial to question where some of Foucault's positions might lead, so it is important to ask what Butler's radical constructivist position proposes and/or elides in its own discursive formation.

Diana Fuss's important contribution to the theorizing of feminist discourse, *Essentially Speaking*, works out of a constructivist position similar to Butler's. But one underlying structure of her discourse is the proposition that constructivism and essentialism rely on and are implicated in each other. Thus, according to Fuss, while constructionists dissolve almost every other fixed notion of self and experience, they maintain an allegiance to politics that is apparently not subject to the same critique. As she says, "To the extent that it is difficult to imagine a *nonpolitical* feminism, politics emerges as feminism's essence" (37). In questioning the "identity politics" of gay and lesbian theory, Fuss likewise uncovers the organizing allegiance to political commitments: "To this extent, paradoxically, politics often occupies an apolitical position in our thinking—a position of unquestioned power and privilege" (105). In drawing out some of the paradoxes concerning the coimplication of gender essentialism and politically oriented constructivism, Fuss's discussion creates ways of understanding both the potential for Foucauldian-style analyses as well as their potential blind spots. By linking my brief examination of Butler's radical constructivist position with Fuss's more synthetic or even conciliatory discussion, I do not mean to set them up as being opposed—in fact, their positions are very similar. Rather, it will be my view that the Foucauldian imperative to conduct our inquiries "at the very limits of ourselves" allows for quite different and varied responses even from those who share political and discursive positions.

The political and discursive position of Elizabeth Meese likewise shares many features with those of Butler and Fuss, but in Meese's case the Foucauldian subtext is almost entirely absent. Rather, Meese's theoretically oriented criticism occupies a position that attempts to maintain the political orientation of feminism, or feminisms, as she prefers to say, through an attention to the moves of Derridean deconstruction. Sounding very much like someone combining Derrida with Foucault, Meese says in *Crossing the Double-Cross*: "Feminist deconstructors argue another view: that the concept of difference empowers claims that women's work has been misrepresented and disregarded. Additionally, they maintain that deconstruction provides theoretical strategies with which feminists can construct a more comprehensive critique of the dominant culture" (79). Meese's more recent work in *(Ex)Tensions* indicates the political impact deconstructive strategies can have when used to investigate questions concerning feminism, but also sexual identity, race, and class. Feminism, in Meese's view, is not singular, but a multiple set of practices, much like deconstruction, and the pragmatic benefits of working in an area that attends to both are very forcefully argued (*(Ex)Tensions*, esp. 24–28).

In this all too brief discussion of the recent work of several theorists working in the areas of theoretical feminism, gender identity, Foucauldian analysis and deconstruction, I have avoided saying that they are lesbian theorists. Such a label limits and substantializes a sexual identity in ways that would be counterproductive, as Butler argues in her article "Imitation and Gender Insurbordination." But clearly, the subject positions each constructs for herself, multiple and shifting as they are, are in some way enabled by constructions of gender and sexuality. My point in discussing their theoretical works in this part of the introduction on Foucault is to show the range of possibilities opened up through attention to sexual and gender identity as a necessary aspect of the contingency of the historical subject. It would be inappropriate for me to imagine that I could speak for such a position or range of positions.[17] But we also need to negotiate critical practices that speak to and across our respective gendered, sexed, class-determined, and racially coded positions. In this way, the work of Foucault has shaped my own discursive position, even when my critical attention is more drawn toward the texts of Derrida and others. There are no simple answers to many of the questions raised about Foucault's practice. His emphasis on power relations can be used to ill effect when his injunction against "global or radical" projects is ignored, leading to a return to the totalizing discourse represented by a universal subject position. My response to other aspects of his work, his focus on sexual identity for example, necessarily involves my own subject positioning in a whole range of societal, cultural, and institutional networks.

Christopher Norris's Postmodern Adventure

When it comes to the task of identifying and putting forth the elements of deconstruction that are useful in establishing what I am here calling the ethical subject of discourse, Christopher Norris's work provides a continuing resource. Norris's range of work on the subject of deconstruction and the principal authors associated with it, notably Derrida and Paul de Man, demonstrates his consistent engagement with their practice. Moreover, Norris has initiated a laudable move to associate the pragmatic and ethical elements in deconstructive practice with other discourses that share its critical function in the social formation. In *What's Wrong with Postmodernism: Critical Theory and the Ends of Philosophy* [WWP] Norris argues for a startling possible alliance between the work of Derrida and the work of Jürgen Habermas, an alliance that promises to demonstrate the socially liberatory dimension of deconstruction in association with Habermas's social praxis philosophy. In order to achieve this potentially powerful theoretical synthesis, Norris must demonstrate the fundamental or underlying sameness of Derrida's and Habermas's theories of language, something that I believe is impossible to do. Norris also constructs an idiosyncratic reading of Derrida's philosophy that dismisses the role of Heidegger's thinking in Derrida's texts while promoting the similarity between Derrida's critical philosophy and that of Paul de Man. The strange move that Norris attempts of avoiding Heidegger's importance to Derridean deconstruction in order to save de Man's theoretical project is similar to the impossible conjunction he constructs between Derrida's and Habermas's theories of language. At the same time, Norris's argument provides a continuing focus for central issues of ethics and critical responsibility related to the practice of deconstruction.

Norris displays an understandable enthusiasm for Habermas's work, *The Philosophical Discourse of Modernity* [PDM], which presents a serious encounter by a representative of the Frankfurt school with the main currents of French poststructuralist thought. Norris character- izes Habermas's work as "an essentially therapeutic exercise" in that Habermas reads the work of Derrida, Lyotard, Baudrillard, and Foucault in a post-Kantian perspective in order to recover what can be recovered for a "large-scale rational reconstruction" (WWP 50).[18] One can see why Norris finds Habermas's work *therapeutic,* since it saves a view of post-Kantian enlightenment philosophy for Norris's purpose, that is, to construct a rationalist praxis-oriented criticism that presents itself as being aware of the main elements of poststructuralism. In order to bring the critical philosophies of Habermas and Derrida together, how- ever, Norris has to account for why Habermas doesn't fully understand Derrida's work. Norris argues: "One reason why *PDM* seems blind to certain aspects of Derrida's work is that it more or less identifies de- construction with the Rortyan-postmodern-pragmatist reading, and thus tends to perpetuate the view of it as a species of literary-critical activ- ity, an attempt to colonise philosophy by levelling the genre-distinction between these disciplines" (WWP 54). If this were the only problem with linking deconstruction to Habermas's discussion of it, or even the main problem, then Norris's critique of Habermas might work to save his attempted synthesis of the two philosophers.

But the differences between Derrida and Habermas run deeper than the leveling of the genre distinction between literature and philosophy of which Habermas accuses Derrida (see PDM 185–210).[19] Their differ- ences extend to their respective theories of language, writing and com- munication. Norris does not emphasize the depth of these differences, since he wants to uphold the rational communicative model of Haber- mas as the basis for his own critical theory. Derrida's deconstruction of the communication model of language and writing is outlined force- fully in "Signature événement contexte," leading to the debate with John Searle that produced *Limited Inc.* Derrida's dismantling of the speech-act model of communication and Habermas's defense of this same model—especially as this is worked out in his critique of Derrida— would prove disastrous to Norris's overall project were he to examine it in any kind of detail. The two models simply cannot be made to con- form and they lead in turn to significantly different theories of the ethics of communication and written discourse.

Habermas argues forcefully for a model of communication based on common or everyday language. He follows the speech-act theorists such as J. L. Austin and John Searle, who believe that such common or everyday usage presents a norm for the description of language, from which other forms of language use can be shown to deviate. Habermas thus puts forth as the standard, the norm of language use, "a mutual understanding in which the *same* utterances are assigned the same meaning." He continues, "As Gadamer has shown, the hermeneutic effort that would bridge over temporal and cultural distances remains oriented toward the idea of a possible consensus being brought about in the present" (PDM 198). Habermas's evidence that the understanding of those engaged in communication is the "same" derives from the speech-act theory of language as performative, since things get done by people based on their linguistic interactions. These are people *"who can act communicatively only under the presupposition of intersubjectively identical ascriptions of meaning"* (PDM 198; italics in the original). I wonder if even the most idealist-oriented philosopher of language could fully assent to Habermas's "intersubjectively identical ascriptions of meaning." What would such an identity mean and how could it be achieved? What exactly does "bridging over" cultural and temporal differences imply in the context of communication? What happens to the *other* in such an exchange? Habermas, who presents himself as a leading philosopher of enlightenment reason and social progress, seems to be missing one of the main ethical strains of postmodern thinking. That is precisely the role of the *other*, not merely as an analogically identical subject, but as unassimilably *different*. In this respect, Habermas remains firmly within an explicitly Kantian paradigm of intersubjective understanding, one that Derrida has repeatedly subjected to intensive scrutiny, especially by concentrating on the analogy of the bridge.[20]

Identity of meaning, even of the subject to him or herself in the moment of utterance, is one focus of Derrida's analyses in SEC. This is the import of Derrida's nonconcept of "iterability" (*itération*): there will always be a nonassimilable remainder (*restance*) that marks the utterance, rendering it other from itself, making the "meaning" other than the "sense" (cf. Llewelyn 60ff.). This *restance* of the utterance is misinterpreted by Searle as a form of permanence in written discourse, when it is in a sense the opposite of permanence, since it allows Derrida to claim that meaning is never "present" in the first place. As Derrida says, "Given that structure of iteration, the intention animating the utterance will never be through and through present to itself and to its content. The iteration structuring it a priori introduces into it a dehiscence and a cleft [*brisure*] which are essential. The 'non-serious,' the *oratio obliqua* will no longer be able to to be excluded, as Austin wished, from 'ordinary' language" (*Limited Inc* 18).[21] Iteration in this usage is very close to Derrida's discussion of the workings of the mark in the operation of *différance*. Here the terms *dehiscence* and *brisure* correspond to the action of differing and deferring. What is important to Derrida's purposes is how this structure of iteration, like that of *différance*, both suspends or interrupts the pure presence of the speaker's intentions *and* introduces (always and already) a programed repetition, meaning that there can be no rigorous distinctions between the "original" or serious utterance and its quoted, even parodic, uses in other contexts. Iteration marks both the structure of the utterance and its surrounding context. This view of language, or writing, is incompatible with Habermas's model, and it is therefore difficult for me to see how Norris can truly understand (or understand and embrace) the structure of iteration as worked out in Derrida's text and still think that there can be a synthesis possible between Derrida and Habermas.

Norris tries hard to argue for Derrida's philosophy as supporting a reason-oriented critique of socio-historical forces. As Norris says (describing his book on Paul de Man), he wants to argue "that deconstruction is a powerful means of understanding what is at stake in the post-romantic treatment of literature as a source of mystified social and political values" (WWP 3). Not only does this involve characterizing Derrida's views on language in such a way as to provoke the uneasy confrontation with Habermas just discussed, Norris must also reorient Derrida's relationship to the immediate philosophical and critical traditions with which deconstruction has been associated. This causes Norris to dismiss the work of Heidegger, particularly as his work could be seen to provide a strong pretext for Derrida's deconstruction, and, paradoxically, to claim Paul de Man as a thinker whose work provides the necessary theorizing of the possible real-world effects of deconstruction. Norris's strategy is designed to show the pragmatic value of deconstruction, its political-ethical force, an area of Derrida's thinking that is often ignored, but which he himself has not hesitated to address. As Derrida says: "Why do people overlook the fact that the exercise of (theoretical and ethico-political) responsibility prescribes that nothing be a priori exempted from the deconstructive questions? Because, in my view, deconstruction consists in nothing less than putting this responsibility to work, especially when it analyzes traditional or dogmatic axioms concerning the concept of responsibility" (*Mémoires* 259n). But this inevitably raises the question of how well Norris, as a praxis-philosopher who argues for deconstruction's real-world effects, exercises his critical responsibility, particularly as a reader of Derrida's and others' texts.

Norris sets up Stanley Fish as the leading representative of the Rortyan pragmatist school, so that he can show the limitations of reader-response theory and the whole range of work by Americans who presumably misunderstand the exact import of Derrida's work (WWP ch. 2).[22] This move allows Norris to express his understanding of the limitations of the hermeneutic circle—thus adumbrating his dismissal of Heidegger's work—and to pose Paul de Man as a counterexample to Fish as someone who understands the real-world effects of deconstruction. According to Norris, Fish reaches the "unwarranted conclusion that reading can do nothing other than confirm those beliefs since they constitute the absolute horizon of intelligibility for each and every act of interpretative grasp" (WWP 114). While I agree with the general sense proposed by Norris that Fish's hermeneutics goes too far in the direction of radical relativism, this does not mean that the hermeneutic circle is always a static entity allowing no escape and no change.[23] Fish's whole enterprise can be seen as an attempt to account for how change can occur within dominant paradigms of understanding and how this can even change the paradigms themselves.[24] Oddly, Norris identifies Paul de Man's theories as supporting "cognitive or truth-seeking interests" left out of Fish's account (WWP 116). Norris argues that de Man's "'epistemology of tropes' . . . opens a space for language to escape the closed circle of interpretative foreknowledge" (WWP 120). Once again, Norris's strategy is difficult to account for here. Somehow cognition and "truth" are seen to exist "outside" the hermeneutic circle, which is interpreted as a static, conservative, unchanging entity.[25] And the means given to effect this escape from "the prison-house of language" is de Man's "epistemology of tropes."[26]

Another important avenue to examine is exactly how Norris drives the wedge between Heidegger's and de Man's positions as they operate in the overall context of what we might heuristically call Derridean deconstruction. Norris uses Philippe Lacoue-Labarthe's text on Heidegger as the basis for what purports to be a fair-minded assessment of Heidegger's work. Norris has serious difficulties with Lacoue-Labarthe's approach, which is based on the idea that one can understand Heidegger's work, and his political stance, only within the context of a detailed understanding of that work. That this would be, and is, Derrida's approach as well, Norris does not mention. Norris says of Lacoue-Labarthe's work: "The trouble with this whole line of argument is that it simply takes over the jargon of authenticity—all the talk of 'essences,' historial *Dasein*, ontological difference and so forth—and uses it as a stick to beat any critic who rejects such mystifying verbiage" (WWP 230). I question whether this characterization of Heidegger's thought—based, of course, on Theodor Adorno's devastating critique in *The Jargon of Authenticity*—can be said to demonstrate basic fairness. Even more disturbing to me is that Norris has claimed a role as a leading interpreter of Derrida, who in turn would seem to be just as prone to such "talk," such as ontological difference, and so forth, as Heidegger engages in. Norris fails to address why this discourse is "mystifying verbiage" when used by Heidegger and socially emancipatory when employed by Derrida.

Norris appears to address some potential aspects of this question when he makes a glancing reference to Derrida's principal work on the political dimensions of Heidegger's thinking: "It seems to me that the real puzzle here is not why so many critics have failed to heed the message of Heidegger's work, but much rather why certain intellectuals—among them thinkers of great acuity and power like Lacoue-Labarthe—should have gone to such lengths of ingenious argumentation by way of protecting that work from any form of reasoned assessment or critique. For it is indeed a striking fact that these defences have often come from thinkers (notably Derrida) whose writing far surpasses Heidegger's own in point of argumentative subtlety and rigour" (WWP 242). First of all, I would dispute the notion that Norris's discussion of Heidegger's "mystifying verbiage," examined previously, constitutes by any measure a "reasoned assessment or critique." But, far more importantly, there is simply no sense in which Derrida's text cited here constitutes a "defense" of Heidegger.

Very briefly stated, Derrida's *De l'esprit* outlines the shift in Heidegger's work from *Sein und Zeit* (1928), in which Heidegger studiously avoids the word *Geist*, to the period of the *Rektoratsrede* and the *Introduction to Metaphysics* (1933), in which Heidegger invokes the specifically German "spirit" as revealed in the "true inner greatness" of National Socialism. Derrida then proceeds to show that this sense of

Geist and its related forms continues to inform Heidegger's thought and that, far from repudiating his previous associations of the word with Nazism, Heidegger continues to evolve a notion of the true nature of *Geist*, particularly as *flame* (*Flamme*), especially in his 1953 essay on Trakl's poetry. Derrida's work is a serious philosophical attempt to understand the socio-historical significance of Heidegger's involvement with Nazism. Among other things, Derrida suggests that there can be no clear us/them distinctions when investigating the intrication of philosophical thinking with socio-historical forces. In my interpretation, Derrida is saying that Nazism, as it derives from philosophy, is so deeply involved in all of the currents of Western philosophy that it is hypocritical to try somehow to stand outside of that tradition and establish a position free of its contamination. Now, it is clear how this movement of thought could threaten an ideologically committed writer such as Norris, but not only does Norris not demonstrate basic fairness to Heidegger's texts, in my view, neither has he exercised his critical responsibility as an interpreter of Derrida.[27]

Fairness and responsibility are very much central terms for Norris, especially in his discussion of the work of Paul de Man. This is especially true since the "de Man affair" would seem to pose some of the same questions regarding de Man's political involvements as those raised in connection with Heidegger.[28] But, in the name of such fairness, Norris claims, "Nobody who has read them would think of comparing de Man's juvenilia (for this is really what they amount to) with anything that Heidegger published either before or after his period of Nazi involvement" (WWP 256). Whether we agree, as I do, with Norris that the writings by the respective figures—Heidegger and de Man—are not of the same level of seriousness, Norris's statement here masks a dilemma with a bare assertion and therefore does not begin to face up to the critical responsibility Norris and I both agree is at the center of these debates. For reading itself carries an inescapable ethical dimension, as de Man's writing demonstrates, and Norris's discussion emphasizes. To those critics of de Man who claim that his later career is an elaborate attempt to disenculpate himself regarding his early experience and writings, Norris has this answer: "That this is a gross misreading of de Man's work—more likely, a determined non-reading—should be clear enough to anyone who has approached that work with a reasonably open, unprejudiced mind" (WWP 259–60). This is undoubtedly true, but I seriously question whether Norris himself exercises this same ethical stance in his critical encounter with Heidegger, which in turn seriously weakens his argument concerning the Heidegger/Derrida relationship.

Norris's insistence on deconstruction's real-world effects in the practice of Derrida and de Man represents an important critical step. Norris is remarkably lucid and convincing when he argues for the Kantian dimension of Derrida's thought and when he deconstructs critics such as John Ellis who oppose deconstruction on the basis of a supposed commonsense approach. Norris's effort to bring Derrida's thinking in line with a Habermasian strain of post-Marxist praxis philosophy simply cannot work, however, despite some clever moves on Norris's part. First of all, any theory that claims to be attentive to Derrida's text and at the same time operates out of a determinable distinction between written texts and the real world is bound to raise serious questions. Second and relatedly, Derrida's work on writing, both in the large sense he gives it in the *Grammatology* and specifically in his discussion of *itération* in SEC, distances him irretrievably from the communication-oriented language theories of Habermas and speech-act theory generally. Third, Derrida *by his own account* remains within an area of thinking opened up by Heidegger, and one therefore cannot dismiss Heideggerian structures of thinking and maintain a viable theory of Derridean deconstruction. I do agree with Norris that critical theory should continue to follow out the ethical dimension of Paul de Man's texts, as this represents an exemplary kind of deconstructive activity, but not by way of the circuitous route Norris maps out in *What's Wrong with Postmodernism*.

Chapter Two

Lacan as a Reader of Merleau-Ponty

Maurice Merleau-Ponty is a prominent French figure in the field of phenomenological analysis and an important, though often unacknowledged, precursor to postmodern thinking on the ethical subject. In the more than thirty years since his death (1961), the explosion of discourse in the fields of ethnology, psychoanalysis, and language theory has led to a far-reaching reexamination of the philosophical tradition. Merleau-Ponty's thinking has been challenged, rejected, or just plain ignored, but there are some at least who feel that his posing of the central questions of the constitution of the body-subject and the relation of that subject to the perceived world deserves to be recognized. Jacques Lacan's close relationship to Merleau-Ponty personally and to his thinking led him to deal with the latter's philosophical questionings at some length in his seminars in the early sixties and, far from rejecting Merleau-Ponty's thinking, Lacan builds on some of the central concepts in Merleau-Ponty's later writings, such as "the flesh of the world," "the intertwining" and "the chiasma" in developing his psychology of the subject.[1] Lacan acknowledges the validity of Merleau-Ponty's investigations in the phenomenological domain, yet tries to show how Merleau-Ponty's analysis of the signifying function falls short, especially in relation to the constitution of the subject. Lacan, in the four lectures of his 1964 *Séminaire* (*The Four Fundamental Concepts of Psychoanalysis*), repeatedly takes up notions in Merleau-Ponty's later philosophy in order to develop his own theory of the "misrecognition of the subject" in its own discourse, thus establishing a key turn for postmodern theories of the subject.

Lacan may well have been one of the first to suggest the notion of Merleau-Ponty as the "last philosopher": "This work, *The Visible and the Invisible,* may indicate for us the moment of arrival of the philosophical tradition" (XI 68; FF, 71). Others have certainly come along to explore what this might mean to our current thinking.[2] For this inquiry, however, the idea of Merleau-Ponty as the "last philosopher" points to a need to review briefly his work as a whole, before trying to develop a more in-depth look at the later works that represent for his thinking a new start. A full introduction to the key concepts of the later philosophy in turn lays the foundation for an examination of their importance to Lacan's theorizing.

Merleau-Ponty's phenomenology, as developed in *The Phenomenology of Perception* (1945), attempts to establish a basis for accurate description of the world as it is lived. Merleau-Ponty rejects both of classical philosophy's antipodes, which he terms empiricism and idealism: of a world that has a physical existence and meaning in the absence of any human subject; and the self-constituting subject that has no direct access to reality. In doing so, Merleau-Ponty follows the lead of Edmund Husserl's investigations into "intentionality."[3] How is it that the world is really there and presents a meaning to us? These two questions are always linked in Merleau-Ponty and together indicate his rejection of classical empiricism. The meaning that the perceived world presents to the perceiving subject is an instance of what Merleau-Ponty terms the *transcendence* of the subject, or the subject's necessary ability to get beyond itself in the act of perception. This represents Merleau-Ponty's rejection of classical idealism and, in the final analysis, of Husserl as well. Merleau-Ponty's project in the *Phenomenology* is thus to follow the threads of intentionality from the perceived world back to the subject. Relying in this work in large measure on previous experiments in *Gestalt* psychology, Merleau-Ponty demonstrates how the overwhelming majority of these intentional orientations are not in the mind, but rather in or of the body. This analysis leads to his striking, and still vital, formulation that *the body is the perceived world* (PP 86; my italics).[4] This concept of the body-subject is central to Merleau-Ponty's phenomenology and constitutes what he feels to be the meeting point between classical empiricism and classical idealism.

Not surprisingly, this conception of the body-subject has met with a great deal of resistance and miscomprehension from both camps. A relatively recent reading from the idealist (he would call himself "analytical" perhaps) philosopher Vincent Descombes shows how Merleau-Ponty's theory can easily be misread. Descombes's analysis of Merleau-

Ponty's phenomenology shows how Merleau-Ponty laid himself open to the idea that he was merely trying to shore up the transcendental, self-positing (or thetic) subject of Husserl—and through Husserl, back to Kant and Descartes. Here is a representative statement by Descombes: "In more general terms, phenomenology maintains that the only meaning which 'being' can have for myself is 'being for myself' [Merleau-Ponty, PP iii], or 'appearing to me'" (Descombes, MA 81; Descombes, MFP 64).[5] If Descombes can slide from Merleau-Ponty's "being for myself" to "appearing to me"—instead of what Merleau-Ponty would have insisted means rather "having a meaning for me" or "giving me a meaning" or, in his later philosophy, "inhabiting me with a meaning"—then it is clear even from this late vantage that Merleau-Ponty's analysis in the *Phenomenology* leads too far in the direction of the idealist subject.[6] To be completely clear that the act of perception is a coming together or linked interdependence of the perceived world and the incarnated subject, Merleau-Ponty in his later philosophy began from the other side, asking the question: what is the quality of the world as it is which allows it to present itself to me complete with a meaning?[7]

"Eye and Mind" (written in 1961) shares many of the same working premises as the unfinished *The Visible and the Invisible* (1964), but in it Merleau-Ponty works out his analyses of them with primary reference to the work and experience of visual artists, painters and sculptors. Merleau-Ponty indicates his new direction early on in the work, when in relation to the *voyant/visible* (or, the one who sees and the visible) paradox he states that "the world is made of the same stuff as the body" (OE 19; EM 163). This anticipates the phrase that appears later—and as a key term in *The Visible and the Invisible*—"the flesh of the world." Merleau-Ponty's concern here is to offer what he calls an "explicitation" of the natural attitude we have towards the world, our "perceptual faith" (VI 17; trans. 3) that means we never question the actual existence of the world in the course of our day-to-day lives. The experience of visual artists becomes important to Merleau-Ponty's thinking because of the "other side" to our natural attitude that their experience makes explicit.

Merleau-Ponty takes up Bernard Berenson's famous idea that painting excites the viewer's tactile sense—and turns it inside-out: "[Painting] gives visible existence to what profane vision believes to be invisible. . . . This voracious vision, reaching beyond the 'visual givens,' opens upon a texture of Being of which the discrete sensorial messages are only the punctuations or the caesurae. The eye lives in this texture as a man lives in his house" (OE 27; EM 166). The sensual experience of the artist—and by extension the viewer—in the painting points not to a totality of experience but to the gaps that make us wonder what all there is. Just the opposite of exciting the viewer's senses, the painting points to that which in the painter's experience—Merleau-Ponty is specifically discussing Paul Cézanne—calls him most out of himself. Merleau-Ponty says about Cézanne's stated feeling of being looked at by what he paints: "It is the mountain itself which from out there makes itself seen by the painter; it is the mountain that he interrogates with his gaze" (OE 28; EM 166). This strong moment in Merleau-Ponty's analysis is the basis for Lacan's extended discussion of "the eye and the gaze" (*l'oeil et le regard*), but I want to remain with Merleau-Ponty to follow out the philosophical implications for his thinking on this subject.

Merleau-Ponty's early phenomenology traced back the threads of intentionality to the body in order to found the subject-object relationship in a nondichotomizing fashion as the body-subject. Even here there were indications of a certain anonymous quality to the body, the "one is able" behind the "I can" (what allows almost any human subject to get behind the wheel of an automobile and drive it, for example). Merleau-Ponty's later philosophy, starting from the other side, asks rather: What characterizes the world's allowing itself to be perceived by the perceiving subject? Merleau-Ponty posits a commonality having its basis in the body between perceived and perceiving. The body is both *seeing/visible, touching/sensible:* the world to come into our perception must likewise have as part of its fundamental nature a perceptive capability; what he calls *flesh* throughout his later writings, as in "the flesh of the world."

So, at the end of "Eye and Mind," he can say, for example: "All flesh, and even that of the world, radiates beyond itself [toute chair, et même celle du monde, rayonne hors d'elle-même]" (OE 81; EM 186). But it would be a serious error to view this concept as a positivistic materialism (at the one extreme) or a religious animism (at the other). What characterizes Merleau-Ponty's philosophy of *flesh* is that it is neither a positive substance, nor a spiritual animism. It is rather the *invisible* that inhabits any *visible*, allowing for the back and forth of perceived-perceiving and ultimately presence-absence. As he says: "Now perhaps we have a better sense of what is meant by that little verb 'to see.' Vision is not a certain mode of thought or presence to self; it is the means given me for being absent from myself, for being present at the fission of Being from the inside—the fission at whose termination, and not before, I come back to myself" (OE 81; EM 186). Here one sees the conceptual force of Merleau-Ponty's later thinking: what from one perspective appears as a certain commonality, "the flesh of the world," is also a fundamental gap or lack, "the fission of Being." Merleau-Ponty's phenomenology seems to have been moving in the direction of the split in the subject that we see in Lacan and other poststructuralist thinkers.

This same dialectic of a commonality, which is yet a kind of split in the subject, drives the more formal analysis in *The Visible and the Invisible*, and finds forceful expression at the end of "Eye and Mind": "Every visual something, as individual as it is, functions also as a dimension, because it gives itself as the result of *a dehiscence of Being* [*une déhiscence de l'Etre*]. What this ultimately means is that the proper essence of the visible is to have a layer of invisibility in the strict sense, which it makes present as a certain absence" (OE 83; EM 187; my italics). While Merleau-Ponty approaches this issue of presence/absence through the act of perception, some of his language—notably his use of *déhiscence*—operates in an area not unlike some of Derrida's analyses. Derrida, however, seeks this play of presence/absence in "writing," which in turn undercuts any "faith" in perceptual experience, and this basic difference between the two philosophers could be seen as a reason for Derrida's almost total silence on the subject of Merleau-Ponty's philosophy. Having examined these hints of Merleau-Ponty's later philosophy in "Eye and Mind," we turn then to the more ambitious, formal analysis in the philosopher's final (and unfinished) work of this dialectic that indicates a new beginning for philosophy from its "last philosopher."

The Visible and the Invisible is often characterized as Merleau-Ponty's attempt to devise a completely new philosophy, complete with a new vocabulary. He is thought to have realized some of the necessary limitations in his earlier work caused by an overreliance on the terminology of Husserl, among others. But just as this unfinished final work introduces terms like *flesh*—which Merleau-Ponty repeatedly insists "has no name in any philosophy" (VI 93; trans. 147)—we also need to be able to recognize the work's continuity with his overall phenomenology. The work begins with an explicit discussion of the "natural attitude" at the basis of phenomenology, what Merleau-Ponty terms "the perceptual faith" (VI 17; trans. 3). Just as he had done in the *Phenomenology*, Merleau-Ponty shows here how an "obscurity" inhabits our relation to the perceived world. Where the earlier phenomenology concentrated on the body-subject's different projections of "intentionality," *The Visible and the Invisible* eventually works from the other side, the side of the perceived world, to show that this obscurity is present in the dialectic of the "flesh of the world" as well. The continuity with the earlier phenomenology is expressed from the outset in the founding of all contact with the perceived world through the body: "It is the perceptual life of my body that here sustains and guarantees the perceptual explicitation, and far from it itself being a cognition of intramundane or interobjective relations between my body and the exterior things, it is presupposed in every notion of an object, and it is this life that accomplishes the primary openness to the world" (VI 60; trans. 37). Merleau-Ponty's goal in this section of the analysis is essentially the same as it was in the *Phenomenology*, the "explicitation" of perceptual relations; so is its grounding in the natural attitude that is inescapably *mine* as an incarnated subject. All "higher" level human activities, such as thinking and reflection, are in turn dependent on this initial "opening to the world" accomplished by and through the body.

The body-subject remains Merleau-Ponty's primary conceptual basis even when he turns to the final (of the chapters that we have) discussion of "The Intertwining—the Chiasma" (VI 172–204; trans. 130–55), which in turn has become the center of focus for subsequent investigations. In terms that both recall the psychological experiments Merleau-Ponty relied on in his early work and show interesting parallels with some of Wittgenstein's inquiries, Merleau-Ponty turns to a discussion of particular examples of color perception (see Wittgenstein, *Philosophical Investigations* and *Remarks on Colour*). Experiments show that the same color is perceived differently depending on the medium or source of the color. Merleau-Ponty's central example is the red dress, the color red of which has a meaning for the perceiving subject that is inextricably linked with it being the red of a dress, a woman who is wearing the dress, and so on. But he wants to claim that the special quality of the "red" in the dress is only a particularly striking example of something latent in all acts of perception; this something he calls *flesh*: "Between the alleged colors and visibles, we would find anew the tissue that lines them, sustains them, nourishes them, and which for its part is not a thing, but a possibility, a latency, and a *flesh* of things [*chair* des choses]" (VI 174–75; trans. 132–33). This double aspect, what Merleau-Ponty calls *flesh*, stems directly from his investigations into the *visible/voyant* paradox that we examined in "Eye and Mind." The *flesh* of things is not some form of animism inherent in things as they are, but the very point of mediation between the things of the world and the body-subject.

The *flesh* of things is the same as the "obscurity" of the body discovered in the earlier phenomenology of perception. As Merleau-Ponty says: "The thickness of the body, far from rivaling that of the world, is on the contrary the sole means I have to go unto the heart of things, by making myself a world and by making them flesh" (VI 178; trans. 135).[8] This is an especially clear example of Merleau-Ponty's attempt to think anew some of the same problems; by developing a new terminology he addresses here once more what he would at one time have termed the *transcendence* of the subject in the act of perception. The back and forth, flux and reflux, involved in the act of perception is what he alternately calls *intertwining* or *chiasma*, both terms for this reciprocity between body-subject and perceived world.

It is perhaps not surprising that this difficult-to-conceptualize move toward a philosophy of *flesh* has been met with a great deal of misunderstanding, even derision.[9] To be completely clear (and also to anticipate Lacan's analysis), I should say that Merleau-Ponty's thinking here, while providing a stimulating and still vital approach to the phenomenology of world and body-subject, does seem particularly weak on the so-called "problem of others" and as a theory of verbal expression. According to Merleau-Ponty, there is no problem of others in the philosophy of *flesh*: "There is here no problem of the *alter ego* because it is not *I* who sees, not *he* who sees, because an anonymous visibility inhabits both of us, a vision in general . . ." (VI 187; trans. 142). In the wake of the subsequent theorizing of Foucault and others (that I discussed in the introduction), it now seems clear that the innocence of intersubjectivity (here a certain "anonymity") based on a pure and neutral perception of the world completely misses the network of power relationships in which human subjects are always already engaged. This problem is related to, though not identical with, the question of linguistic expression. When he speaks, Merleau-Ponty says, he becomes "a sonorous being [un être sonore]" (VI 190; trans. 144). So the same analysis of *flesh*, from this perspective, should also be possible for linguistic phenomena: "It is as though the visibility that animates the sensible world were to emigrate . . . as though it were to change flesh, abandoning the flesh of the body for that of language" (VI 200; trans. 153). I shall now turn to Lacan's analysis of the shortcomings of this evaluation of language as corporal gesture, and just note that at this time Derrida's investigation into the same problem in Husserl's phenomenology was to establish a basis for a thoroughgoing "deconstruction" of the Western metaphysics of presence (examined in detail in the next chapter) which Merleau-Ponty's thinking presupposes.[10]

Just after Merleau-Ponty's sudden death in 1961, Jacques Lacan contributed an article to a special issue of *Les Temps modernes,* "Maurice Merleau-Ponty" (TM; REPP). It is at once a eulogy and a critique, and demonstrates well both Lacan's respect for Merleau-Ponty the man and the philosopher and the key differences in their respective theories. Lacan, in the first instance, seems to indicate his assent to Merleau-Ponty's phenomenology as a ground for explaining the body-subject and the act of perception. When he turns to Merleau-Ponty's ideas on the constitution of the thinking and speaking subject, Lacan notes his own difference in approach based on what he calls psychoanalysis's access to the signifier. As a result of the dominance of the signifier—in Lacan's view—the subject as such is always "primordially repressed" (TM 251, REPP 78). Given this initial divergence, the problems with Merleau-Ponty's theory of speech as corporal gesture are even more evident, from the psychoanalytical perspective. In other words, since the subject is under the dominance of the signifier there can be no possibility of its speech as mere extension of corporal gesture.[11] Just the reverse in fact is true: the subject's speech as it constitutes the verbal "I" shows that whatever "thought" is present is *not* where it comes to appear.[12] Subsequent critics have generally accepted this as Lacan's refutation of Merleau-Ponty's thinking, due to the latter's misunderstanding of the full significance of the Freudian unconscious.[13] In this article, however, Lacan indicates that Merleau-Ponty's investigations into the "invisible" in "Eye and Mind" "show enough that Maurice Merleau-Ponty moves forward here to a field different from that of perception" (TM 253, REPP 79). What in this article Lacan frames as "merely a comment" is exactly the area he investigates in his *Séminaire XI (The Four Fundamental Concepts of Psychoanalysis).* Though Lacan finds Merleau-Ponty's phenomenology inadequate from the perspective of the problem of others and particularly in regard to the function of language in the constitution of the subject, it is clear that, for Lacan, Merleau-Ponty broaches important questions regarding the subject's relation to the visual field of perception and the "non-objective" or "invisible" dimension to which such an inquiry points.

Lacan's return to an extended discussion of Merleau-Ponty, over the period of four weeks in his *Séminaire* of 1964 (XI 65–109; FF 67–119), shows just how deeply his own thinking is indebted to that of his colleague and friend. These four lectures move from the discussion of Freud's concept of repetition to a preparation for discussing transference as it takes place in the analytical setting. The whole analysis turns on a discussion of what Lacan terms "the scopic dimension" (XI 105; FF 114), and for its central moment, he looks to the indications of Merleau-Ponty's later philosophy. As he says: "What we have to circumscribe, by means of the path he indicates for us, is the pre-existence of a gaze— I see only from one point, but in my existence I am looked at from all sides" (XI 69; FF 72). The idea that Merleau-Ponty derived from his investigation into the experience of painters—that the mountain was watching Cézanne, calling him somehow to respond through his artistic activity—Lacan assents to, but in order to investigate its importance in the constitution of the subject from the psychoanalytical perspective.

Aside from the extreme respect Lacan accords to the work of Merleau-Ponty in this initial invocation, it is interesting to note here some of Lacan's hints concerning the limitations of his own analysis. Still in relation to Merleau-Ponty's phenomenology, Lacan frankly states: "What I try to outline in my discourse . . . makes no claim to cover the entire field of experience. Even this between-the-two [*entre-deux*] that opens up for us the apprehension of the unconscious is of concern to us only in as much as it is designated for us, through the instructions Freud left us, as that of which the subject has to take possession" (XI 69; FF 72). If we were to divide (arbitrarily, of course) the field of human experience into: (1) the body-subject and its experience of the perceived world; (2) the subject's relation to others; and (3) the constitution of the subject in its own discourse, it seems clear from context that Lacan has no argument with Merleau-Ponty's theory of (1), and from the above statement that Lacan himself is not interested in exploring (1) or even (2), except insofar as (1) and (2) impinge on (3), which henceforth becomes his sole topic. In other words, Lacan accepts the phenomenological "explicitation" of the body-subject as perceived world; questions, but ultimately brackets, phenomenology's explanation of the subject's relation to others; and takes from Merleau-Ponty's ideas on the "invisible" dimension of lived experience a direction in exploring what we might call the "psychology of the individual," were it only so simple. Lacan's own description of his project is as follows: "The gaze [*Le regard*] is presented to us only in the form of a strange contingency, symbolic of what we find on the horizon, as the thrust of our experience, namely, the lack that constitutes castration anxiety. The eye and the gaze [*L'oeil et le regard*]—this is for us the split in which the drive is manifested at the level of the scopic field" (XI 69–70; FF 72–73). It will take Lacan most of the four lectures to make it from the *gaze* to castration anxiety, but here at least he makes explicit his divergence from Merleau-Ponty. From the paired terms *eye/mind* or *visible/invisible*, Lacan moves to *eye/gaze*. Clearly then, the *gaze* is the operative term in the psychic mechanism Lacan wishes to explore, specifically *the gaze of the Other* (*le regard de l'Autre*), of which one might say: "I am as I am in the gaze of the Other."

Never one to make things simple, Lacan from here plunges right into a discussion of the biological phenomenon of mimicry (*mimétisme*), and specifically that of ocelli (*sing.* ocellus). Ocelli are the false eyes that are a feature on many butterflies and which, at least according to Lacan's information in 1964, do not seem to serve any protective or camouflage function. What are they there for? He inquires: "it is a question of understanding whether [ocelli] impress . . . by their resemblance to the eyes, or whether, on the contrary, the eyes are fascinating only by virtue of their relation to the form of the *ocelli*. In other words, must we not distinguish between the function of the eye and that of the gaze?" (XI 70; FF 73–74). First off, Merleau-Ponty would have appreciated the rhetorical *chiasmus* Lacan employs here (cf. Schmidt 31 *passim*). It may be that Lacan is even paying a sort of stylistic tribute to Merleau-Ponty, although Lacan's propensity to this trait of style is likewise marked.[14] In fact, we are dealing here with an example of Merleau-Ponty's notion of *chiasma* (VI 268, 316–17; trans. 214–15, 263–64), or the interdependence or "crossing" of body-subject and perceived world. Essential to the philosophy of *flesh*, this crisscrossing in the act of perception leads Merleau-Ponty to hypothesize the world's perceptive capability.

Lacan takes this insight into the mutual constitution of subject and world in a different direction altogether. If he is interested in the subject's sentiment of being looked at by the world, it is for what this says about the constitution of the subject. He makes this explicit: "I mean, and Maurice Merleau-Ponty points this out, that we are beings who are looked at, in the spectacle of the world [*le spectacle du monde*]. That which makes us consciousness institutes us by the same token as *speculum mundi*. Is there no satisfaction of being under that gaze of which, following Merleau-Ponty, I spoke just now, that gaze that circumscribes us, and which in the first instance makes us beings who are looked at, but without showing this?" (XI 71; FF 74–75]. Lacan obviously makes reference to his "mirror stage" theory ("*Le stade du miroir comme formateur de la fonction de Je*," *Écrits*, 93–100]. But the global feeling of being looked at is something not even that theory develops in explicit fashion. And what about the butterfly we left a while back? Lacan, in one of those brilliant turns that make him a sage to some and a madman to others, proceeds to introduce the story of Chuang-tsu's dream, "In a dream, he is a butterfly" (XI 72; FF 76]. Beware, Lacan warns us: the Wolf-Man's wasp phobia is not far off. When Chuang-tsu awakes he is left with the feeling he might now be a butterfly dreaming he is Chuang-tsu.[15] Which, according to Lacan, proves he is not crazy. Why not? Here is Lacan's analysis:

> This is proved by the fact that, when he is the butterfly, the idea does not occur to him to wonder whether, when he is Chuang-tsu awake, he is not the butterfly that he is dreaming of being. This is because, when dreaming of being the butterfly he will no doubt have to bear witness later that he represented himself as a butterfly. But this does not mean that he is captivated by the butterfly— he is a captive butterfly, but captured by nothing, for, in the dream, he is a butterfly for nobody. It is when he is awake that he is Chuang-tsu for others, and is caught in their butterfly net.
>
> This is why the butterfly may—if the subject is not Chuang-tsu, but the Wolf Man—inspire in him the phobic terror of recognizing that the beating of little wings is not so very far from the beating of causation, of the primal stripe marking his being for the first time in the grid of desire. (XI 72–73; FF 76]

This passage works on many levels simultaneously, managing at least allusively to connect the *gaze* of the world (or *Other*] with the false eyes of the butterfly, the "dream" of self-identity and the Wolf-Man's castration complex. Let us be clear: for Lacan, the *gaze* is an object (what he calls *objet a*]; this object is the object of the subject's desire;

and this structure is what ensures that the subject is *the one who does not see.*

How can the gaze (or *le regard*) be an "object" in Lacan's terminology? In the next lecture he turns to a discussion of this "*objet a*": "In the scopic relation, the object upon which the fantasm depends, and from which the subject is suspended in an essential vacillation, is the gaze. Its privilege—and also that by which the subject for so long has been misunderstood as being in its dependence—derives from this very structure" (XI 78–79; FF 83 [trans. modified]). The fantasm, for Lacan, is the essential structure of the Imaginary realm. Based on the mirror stage, which in turn is based on Freud's theory of narcissism, the Imaginary realm is the realm of the subject's desire. Since the Imaginary relation is not in any sense Real, nor does it have any access to the Symbolic realm of language and signification, except indirectly— an endless vacillation in the Imaginary realm, for Lacan, means psychic stasis and ultimately paralyzing mental illness. But the Imaginary structure as that by which the subject—in relation to the "objet a"— constructs its fantasm, is the underlying, always-present activity of desire, desire of the Other, which in turn subtends all human activity.

The fundamental character of desire, then, is that desire is of (or for) the Other, and signals the necessary misrecognition by the subject of itself in the Imaginary realm. Lacan's *gaze of the Other* (*regard de l'Autre*) should not be confused with Jean-Paul Sartre's "*regard d'autrui*," which for Sartre is a strong moment in the constitution of the self-positing (or thetic) subject (*L'Etre et le néant*, 298–349). Lacan addresses this directly: "The gaze I encounter—you can find this in Sartre's own writing—is, not a seen gaze, but a gaze imagined by me in the field of the Other" (XI 79; FF 84). Sartre sets the scene with the voyeur looking through the keyhole who is then himself caught in the gaze of an other. But as Lacan notes, even the sound of a footstep is enough to trigger the voyeur's guilty response (and subsequently, the wish to annihilate the other). What Sartre overlooks in the structure of the gaze is *exactly* the role of desire (XI 80; FF 85).

In order to give an example of the gaze as an object of desire, Lacan introduces the topic of anamorphosis, specifically in reference to Hans Holbein's painting, *The Ambassadors* (XI 80–83; FF 85–89). Lacan here comes straight out (instead of his usual practice which, as he says, is not to let the audience see his cards) and announces that the "floating object" at the foreground of Holbein's famous painting has an inescapable phallic quality (loaf of bread, melted watch, call it what you will). Yet the ideal observer who is walking away from the painting catches through the corner of his/her eye the desired representation, that of a death's head, or skull. For Lacan, this is the exact structure, the perfect representation, of the "*minus-phi* of castration" as the limit of the Imaginary (XI 83; FF 89). But anamorphosis is not merely a special trick for Lacan—it represents the essential structure of the visual, perceptive field: the subject is inescapably bound by its own limited vantage point (the here and now), which in turn is a product of desire (cf. "Kant avec Sade," E 765–90). We're back to Merleau-Ponty's philosophy of *flesh*.

Lacan makes this idea explicit when he returns to the topic of anamorphosis in his next lecture: "In this matter of the visible, everything is a trap, and in a strange way—and is shown very well by Maurice Merleau-Ponty in the title of one of the chapters of *The Visible and the Invisible—entrelacs* (interlacing, intertwining). There is not a single one of the divisions, a single one of the double sides that the function of vision presents, that is not manifested to us as a labyrinth. As we begin to distinguish its various fields, we always perceive more and more the extent to which they intersect" (XI 86–87; FF 93). And then, after some more technical discussion, and almost as if to join ranks one last time with Merleau-Ponty, Lacan tells a personal anecdote about a can of sardines (XI 88–89; FF 95–96). In his twenties, he's knocking around, Lacan says, with no other thought than to go out fishing in his native Brittany. One day while they're out on the boat, a kid called Petit-Jean notices a sardine can floating on the water and jokes to Lacan: "*You see that can? Do you see it? Well, it doesn't see you*" (XI 89; FF 95). But instead of thinking this is funny, Lacan is made uneasy by the joke. He explains why: "To begin with, if what Petit-Jean said to me, namely, that the can did not see me, had any meaning, it was because in a sense, it was looking at me, all the same. It was looking at me at the level of the point of light, the point at which everything that looks at me is situated—and I am not speaking metaphorically" (XI 89; FF 95). We are beings who are looked at, gazed at, regarded; this structure is fundamental to what it means to be human. Lacan has turned the finger of the glove inside out, but the idea itself he took from Merleau-Ponty.[16]

It is the nature of discourse—and of the linguistic sign itself in the working of the *trace,* in Derrida's formulation—to cover its origins.

Many of the French theorists of structuralism and poststructuralism over the past thirty years owe more than they often care to admit to the later philosophy of Merleau-Ponty and to phenomenology in general. In the course of this study, some of the limitations of his work have emerged. It is unclear how his philosophy of *flesh* can account for "the problem of others," which is a key theme of Emmanuel Levinas (see chapter 4). Despite an ongoing interest in Saussure, Merleau-Ponty seems to have been unable to develop a rigorous theory of verbal signification. Language as an extension of corporal gesture, from this "late" vantage, seems naive as a theory. Yet the thorough, provocative, and tantalizing discourse of Lacan, like a series of jazz improvisations on a theme by Merleau-Ponty, shows just how seriously Lacan as a thinker took Merleau-Ponty's later philosophy. *We are beings who are looked at.* Whether the world has this perceptive capability, or *flesh*, that Merleau-Ponty attributes to it, or whether this structure is to be located in the Imaginary realm of desire, as Lacan would have it, the formulation speaks to our essential human condition. Ultimately, I would say that it is not possible to distinguish these two positions. There is no point outside of the Imaginary from which one could establish an "objective" view of the world. This is what Merleau-Ponty's philosophy points to and Lacan's psychoanalytic theory confirms in the realm of the subject. The language of the current critical discourse has moved strongly towards conceptual models based on difference and exteriority. For these terms to continue to make sense to us as human beings, it may be advisable to continue seeking to understand Merleau-Ponty's *chiasma*, or commonality between body-subject and perceived world, that allows for difference and exteriority to come into view.

Chapter Three

Derrida and the Theory of Difference

The rise of structuralist-poststructuralist theory in the sixties and seventies is intricately linked to currents in phenomenology, as the relationship of Lacan to the thinking of Merleau-Ponty in the previous chapter has shown. One critic has called the work of Gilles Deleuze and Jacques Derrida on difference "the radicalization of phenomenology" (Descombes, MA 160; MFP 135). Just as Merleau-Ponty developed important elements of his philosophy starting from Husserl's phenomenology, so Heidegger is an important precursor to both Deleuze and Derrida—particularly Heidegger's writing on difference from the fifties. Heidegger's philosophy of difference is generally interpreted as a philosophy of the Same, in the sense that what is Identical does not change, whereas the Same is able to incorporate and/or reveal difference. The key question for Heidegger is the ontological difference between Being and beings and it is this question much of his work from this period addresses. Deleuze's major work on difference, *Différence et répétition* (1967), recasts the question adroitly to pair difference with repetition, bringing in the Kantian categories of time and iterability. As far as Deleuze goes, he remains, in this work at least, within a certain post-Kantian philosophical tradition. Derrida's work on difference, or *différance* as he terms it in his well-known neologism, seeks to demonstrate, if not the end, at least the closure of metaphysical thinking. *Différance* in this project is neither word nor concept, but what underlies language, writing and thinking generally, enabling them without being restricted by what can be thought within their scope. Derrida's project then is perhaps the most "radical" way of thinking or unthinking difference and this movement continues to play an important role in Derrida's more recent writings.

Heidegger's work on difference takes its place in an explicitation of Being as presence, in order to be able to ask the fundamental questions: How do beings differ from Being? How do there come to be beings? Why should there be beings instead of nothing at all? This line of ontological question—indeed, for Heidegger, the question of beings and Being is *the* ontological question—forgotten in the course of development of Western philosophy, can be seen as a "search for origins."[1] One aspect of this search is Heidegger's persistent return to the thinking of the pre-Socratics. His famous interpretation of the phrase of Parmenides concerning Being may stand as paradigmatic of this search. Heidegger renders the phrase: "Thinking and Being belong together in the Same and by virtue of the same" (ID 27, 90). In Heidegger's philosophy, it is the human subject (or *Dasein*) who, thinking, allows Being to become present. This attempt at thinking Heidegger also terms openness: "For it is man, open towards Being, who alone lets Being arrive as presence" (31, 95). What is important in Heidegger's philosophy of Being as presence is the difference between Identity and the Same. In fact, it is difference, as such, that allows for the Same, that allows the human subject to think the Same instead of remaining trapped in a sterile play of Identity.

In a famous digression in his essay on poetry from 1951, "Poetically Man Dwells," Heidegger states: "We can only say 'the same' if we think difference" (218). Mark Taylor comments on this phrase: "To think what philosophy leaves unthought, one must think difference *as* difference rather than as covert or implicit identity. Difference *as* difference necessarily entails a separating that is a joining and a joining that is a separating. This difference that simultaneously divides and gathers is what Heidegger means by the 'same'" (A 20).[2] Moreover Heidegger argues that "it is in the carrying out and settling of differences that the gathering nature of sameness comes to light. The same banishes all zeal always to level what is different into the equal or identical. The same gathers what is distinct into an original being-at-one" (218–19). Thus it is clear that the Same (*das Selbe*) is not the identical and that difference, as such, is what allows the same to appear. Heidegger will take up this line of thinking again in his essay on Hegel's theory of difference, "The Onto-Theological Constitution of Metaphysics," from 1957 (ID, 42–74; 107–43).

In this lecture, some of Heidegger's most pressing statements on difference concern the necessary effort to think through a previous philosopher's work in the "same" way.³ In the context of his "conversation" with Hegel concerning thinking, Heidegger states: "But the same is not merely the identical. In the merely identical, the difference disappears. In the same the difference appears, and appears all the more pressingly, the more resolutely thinking is concerned with the same matter in the same way [Allein das Selbe ist nicht das Gleiche. Im Gleichen verschwindet die Verschiedenheit. Im Selben erscheint die Verschiedenheit]" (ID 45, 110). In a way that anticipates both Deleuze's and Derrida's call for a nonconceptual approach to difference, Heidegger distinguishes his thinking from Hegel's as from a thinking in terms of conceptual logic, "the idea as absolute concept. For us . . . the matter of thinking is the difference *as* difference [Fur uns ist die Sache des Denkens . . . die Differenz *als* Differenz]" (47, 113). One crucial difference that emerges in just this brief review of Heidegger's complex treatment of the issue is a progressive terminological shift. From *der Untershied* or *der Unter-shied*, the term that he uses in the 1951 lecture on Trakl (already the hyphen in the latter pointing to a working through of the term to radicalize its root meaning), to the two terms above, both translated as "difference," *die Verschiedenheit* and *das Differenz*, one notes a progression from the more common term to a more unusual one that emphasizes the verbal or productive aspect.⁴ Difference *as* difference (*Differenz*) seems to point to a nonconceptualizing move, a move that would investigate what precedes, or allows for, conceptual thought.

This move to a nonconceptual difference is what Heidegger seems to mean by the "step back" (*der Schritt zurück*), as when he says: "We speak of the *difference* between Being and beings. The step back goes from what is unthought, from the difference as such, into what gives thought. That is the *oblivion* of the difference [Wir sprechen von der *Differenz* zwischen dem Sein und dem Seienden. Der Schritt zurück geht vom Ungedachten, von der Differenz als solcher, in das zu-Denkende. Das ist die *Vergessenheit* der Differenz]" (50, 116). Subsequent writers, Deleuze and Derrida in particular, have offered critical interpretations of this philosophy of the Same. What is important to insist on here is the nonconceptualizing grounding, or nonoriginary originating nature of Heidegger's difference. Within the metaphysical framework, Heidegger says, what can be said of difference is: "What differs shows itself as the Being of beings in General, and as the Being of beings in the Highest" (70, 139). Yet where this difference comes from, its origin, cannot be reached by following through metaphysical thinking: "The origin of the difference can no longer be thought within the scope of metaphysics" (71, 140). Undoubtedly, Heidegger's philosophy is one of Presence, thought of as the Same, and giving a unique privilege to language as humankind's way of access to Being. Yet in radicalizing difference, Heidegger already points to the closure of metaphysics that subsequent writers will explore.

Gilles Deleuze, in his 1967 study, *Différence et répétition*, adroitly places difference in the post-Kantian context of repetition, as the title alone suggests, in order to avoid what he views as the pitfalls of Hegel's and Heidegger's philosophy of difference.[5] Placing difference in the context of repetition and the transcendental category of time allows Deleuze considerable conceptual power as he follows through his extremely intricate analysis. Descombes has summarized well the import of this move: "This is why phenomena of repetition are a privileged means of access to a more authentic understanding of difference, because they offer the example of an incontestable, but apparently inconceivable, difference. We must therefore stop defining repetition as the return of the same, as the reiteration of the identical: repetition is, quite the contrary, the *production* (in both senses of the word: to cause to exist, and to show) of difference" (MA 180; MFP 154). Working the two principles of difference and repetition back through the one and the other allows Deleuze to demonstrate this *productive* aspect of difference that Descombes identifies as central to his argument. This in turn enables Deleuze to criticize strongly the thinking of difference that remains within what he calls the system of representation.

Beginning at least with Plato, Deleuze argues, repetition is viewed as a secondary phenomenon, a *simulacrum* to be viewed with suspicion and mistrust. In the philosophy of representation, the key moment is one of recognition that invokes the adequation of thought to certain hypotheses taken as starting points (DR 253–54). Up to and including Hegel, this movement from hypothesis to self-evidence necessarily places repetition (and thus difference) in a position where it will always be misconstrued and undervalued. In a subtle turn, Deleuze proposes that "the movement does not go from the hypothetical to the apodictic, but from the problematic to the question" (DR 255). Backing up this (textual) practice Deleuze adduces Mallarmé ("Un coup de dés") and Joyce as literary examples, but relies primarily on Nietzsche and the "eternal return" as a model that breaks with the philosophy of representation.

Having given an outline of Deleuze's position and a brief overview of his relation to the philosophical tradition, we must turn to a more careful analysis of the specific steps of his argument. That means returning initially to repetition. Repetition, he claims, has been misrepresented, ignored, and passed over in the philosophical tradition, emerging in the (marginal) forms of irony and humor (12), especially in the works of Kierkegaard and Nietzsche. Repetition also reveals a certain "blockage" in mental processes, such as those analyzed by Freud (27ff.). Repetition as a noncognitive (or "unconscious") phenomenon thus appears as a nonconceptual difference. Deleuze states: "After all, repetition is difference without concept. But in the first instance, difference is only proposed as exterior to the concept, falling into the indifference of space and of time. But in the other instance, difference is interior to the Idea: it is deployed as a pure movement creating dynamic space and time that correspond to the Idea. The first repetition is the repetition of the Same, which is explained by the identity of the concept and the representation; the second is that which comprehends difference, and comprehends itself in the otherness of the Idea, in the heterogeneity of an 'appresentation'" (36). The former kind of difference would seem to be the Hegelian difference, which ultimately is a form of "indifference" or Identity.[6] The latter type of nonconceptual difference results from the productive repetition identified earlier and, according to Deleuze, cannot be thought within the philosophy of representation.

Deleuze also claims that Heidegger's philosophy of difference remains finally within representational thinking. In a long footnote, "Note on Heidegger's philosophy of difference" (89–91), Deleuze develops a five-part analysis of Heidegger's thought; he ends with the judgment that Heidegger propounds a philosophy of "univocal being," the final proof of this being Heidegger's misestimation of Nietzsche's eternal return. At the very end of his study, Deleuze returns to this critique of Heidegger (citing "Poetically Man Dwells"), saying: "This is why the philosophy of Difference seems to us poorly established, as long as one is content to oppose terminologically, to the platitude of the Identical as equal to itself, the profundity of the Same that is supposed to recuperate the different" (384). This represents Deleuze's most pointed criticism of Heidegger's philosophy of difference. Heidegger's philosophy remains caught within representational thinking, Deleuze claims, in that the philosophy of the Same displays the same movement from hypothesis to self-evidence that dominates the Western tradition from Plato to Hegel.

We need to look closely at the second type of difference identified above, that difference "within the Idea," produced by an active repetition. In the context of a discussion of Kant's difference from Descartes in their theories concerning the constitution of the subject (the introduction of time as a transcendental, a priori category), Deleuze discusses Kant's distinction between "the determinable" (the specific instance) and "the Determinant" (the general, or transcendental, category). This is a special, productive instance of the "internal difference" within the Idea: "This third category is sufficient to make logic a transcendental instance. It constitutes the discovery of Difference, no longer as an empirical difference between two discernments, but transcendental Difference between THE discernment and that which it discerns—no longer as exterior difference which separates, but internal Difference, and which *a priori* relates being to thinking and *vice versa*" (116). One sees here not only the importance of Deleuze's post-Kantian position, but the power this distinction brings to Deleuze's approach to a non-conceptual difference. Rather than being contained *within* the philosophy of identity or opposition, this "interior" difference precedes and establishes the possibility for opposition and identity. Deleuze states: "*Opposition, resemblance, identity and even analogy are only effects produced by these presentations of difference,* instead of being the underlying conditions of difference, that make it something represented" (189; italics in the original). The result of this shift is a major overhaul of many of the vaunted conceptual positions founded on difference. One example is the famous linguistic concept of "difference" proposed by Saussure, which Deleuze attacks as being merely a weak version of difference founded on opposition, and which becomes a primary point for analysis by Derrida in the *Grammatology*.

In conclusion, then, Deleuze recapitulates the four areas in which difference has been misunderstood in the philosophy of representation; the four categories themselves are taken from Foucault, as he acknowledges (Deleuze, DR 337; see Foucault, *Les Mots et les choses*). The first is to restore the place of difference in thinking, breaking the identity of the concept and the thinking subject (342). The second is to restore "difference within intensity, as the being of the perceived" (342). This, as we have seen, is accomplished through the Kantian distinction between the determinable and the Determinant.[7] Third, Deleuze attempts, as we have seen, to restore "the differential within the Idea" (345), and here particularly he sets out his difference from the negative of Hegel: "This breaks the false link which subordinates difference to the negative" (345; cf. 344). Finally, the cumulative effect of productive repetition and internal difference is to place into serious question "the analogy of judgment" (345 ff.). With productive repetition undermining the consistency of the judging subject, and internal difference breaking down representational thinking on which hypotheses, conclusions, and judgments are based—in Deleuze's view—a new model of the judging subject is inevitable. The fact that Deleuze in this work attains such far-reaching conclusions, while remaining within a certain limiting vocabulary and post-Kantian "doctrine of the faculties," particularly as regards the sensible (or *le donné*), points to this as a limited study.[8] His more recent works show the radical shift Deleuze's thought has since taken (notably his works coauthored with Felix Guattari). Here it remains to investigate the way Derrida, operating from many of the same premises and against some of the same philosophical currents, proposes even more radical measures.

In Derrida's 1967 study of Husserl's theory of expression, *La voix et le phénomène* (*Speech and Phenomena*), there is already a marked difference from Deleuze in the delimitation of Derrida's field of inquiry. We have seen, in a very limited way, some of the problems Deleuze becomes involved in with his discussion of the sensible (or *le donné*), including a reliance on a post-Kantian framework and vocabulary. In this relatively early work of Derrida, the choice to concentrate specifically on Husserl's theory of expression may seem a purely "strategic" one (as he often states in other contexts). By driving the wedge of *différance* into the subject's own "self-understanding," or *s'entendre-parler* (literally, "hearing oneself speak"), Derrida is well on his way to undermining the very structure of perception and experience which phenomenology, up to and including Merleau-Ponty, sets as its main task to investigate.[9] How the speaking subject understands him or herself, how meaning is or is not communicated in an utterance, the "expressive layer" that Husserl introduces to explain these questions—all of these will be subjected to intense scrutiny by Derrida. The resulting (or founding) difference, or *trace*, he discovers will become an operative term in his overall project of deconstruction.

For Heidegger, language is the place where the human subject encounters Being.[10] For Husserl, language enters into the project of a phenomenological description of experience as an added layer to the self-understanding of the subject in the act of communication. Derrida shows deftly that Husserl's theory of expression is both an afterthought, or *supplément, and* the kernel of his theory of meaning. While described overtly as a relatively insignificant part of the constitution of the phenomenological subject (or transcendental subject), metaphors concerning speech and language are elsewhere used to shore up key moves that otherwise might be resistant to explication. Derrida sees very well that language (say, as opposed to the sensible or the givens of perception that occupy Deleuze's analysis of repetition) is the realm of difference; he also realizes that this difference has never been properly recognized; and he will claim that this nonconceptual difference, or *différance,* in fact points up the necessary limitations of phenomenology as any "metaphysical" system of philosophy. Concerning the central place of language in his analysis, Derrida states: "It is at the price of this war of language against itself that the sense and question of its origin will be thinkable. This war is obviously not one war among many. A polemic for the possibility of sense and of world, it takes its place within this *difference* which, as we have seen, cannot reside in the world, but only language, in the transcendental disquietude of language. Indeed, far from only living in language, difference is also its origin and home. *Language maintains the difference which maintains language"* (VP 13; trans. 14 modified; final italics mine). In a sense, then, Derrida has already adduced as his justification for investigating this area of Husserl's discourse a quasi-Heideggerian advance in the theory of phenomenology. When the central moment of Husserl's system—the transcendental reduction—comes under examination, this will be reinterpreted in terms of language and thus Husserl's theory of expression.

Husserl's theory of expression stems from a distinction he adapts from Gottlob Frege between *Sinn* (sense) and *Bedeutung* (meaning). Derrida translates the verb *bedeuten* as "vouloir-dire" ("means to say") and the noun *Bedeutung* as "*ce que* quelqu'un ou un discours *veulent dire"* ("*that which* someone or a discourse *means to say")* or *meaning* (VP 18; trans. 18 modified). This "expressivity" of a discourse is thus paradoxically not simply the inner idea of the speaking subject, but the exteriorization of that idea. And yet the transcendental or phenomenological reduction has theoretically bracketed any other subjectivity toward which such a discourse might be addressed. As Derrida says: "By a strange paradox, the *vouloir-dire* does not isolate the concentrated purity of its *ex-pressivity* until the moment when the relation with a certain outside is suspended" (VP 22; trans. 22 modified). By bringing a theory of expression into the constitution of the transcendental subject, Husserl opens a breach which Derrida will exploit freely. To the purity of the transcendental reduction will always correspond the supplement of language or expression. As Derrida says, "transcendental phenomenological idealism answers to the necessity to describe the *ob*jectivity of the *ob*ject (*Gegenstand*) and the *pre*sence of the *pre*sent (*Gegenwart*)—and objectivity within presence—starting from an 'interiority' or rather a proximity to oneself, of an *ownness* [*propre*] (*Eigenheit*) that is not a simple *within* [*dedans*], but the intimate possibility of a relation to an over-there and to an outside in general" (VP 23; trans. 22 modified).

One consequence of the above paradox of a meaning "exteriorized" in the theoretical absence of any possible interlocutor is the strange specter of meaning as an internal "soliloquy." One must also face the question of how to move from "experience" to the creation of meaning. At this stage Derrida, very much as we have seen with Deleuze, exploits the uncertain status of repetition in the theory of representation. The self-presence of hearing oneself speak depends on a unity in the subject between *presence* (of the subject to itself) and *representation* (of experience to the subject) or *Vorstellung*. This *presence* Derrida shows to be a thoroughly metaphysical idea: "But this ideality, which is but another name for the permanence of the same and the possibility of its repetition, *does not exist* in the world, and it does not come from another world. It depends entirely on the possibility of acts of repetition. It is constituted by repetition. Its 'being' is only measured by the power of repetition. . . . To think presence as the universal form of transcendental life is to open myself to the knowledge that in my absence, beyond my empirical existence, before my birth and after my death, *the present is*" (VP 58, 60; trans. 52, 54 modified). This is one of those moments in reading Derrida's text when the reader is forced either to demur or to face a vertiginous falling away of the ground on which the traditional understanding of the subject is based. What is clear is that there is a gap between self-presence and the self-representation of experience to oneself. The weakness of Husserl's system becomes yet more apparent when the philosopher tries to shore up this gap with a questionable sleight-of-hand.

Husserl's sleight-of-hand is, according to Derrida, to claim retention (of experience or perception) as originary perception (VP 67–73; trans. 60–65). As we have seen previously in the analysis of Deleuze, this move is not atypical of the misrecognition or discounting of repetition generally in the philosophy of representation. Derrida insists on this point and, in doing so, opens the breach for a far more radical critique than Deleuze's. On retention as originary perception, Derrida states: "As soon as one admits this continuity of the now and the not-now, of perception and non-perception in a zone of originarity common to both the original impression and its retention, one lets the other into the identical-to-itself of the *Augenblick*: non-presence and lack-of-evidence into the *wink of an eye of the instant*. There is a duration to the wink of an eye; and it closes the eye. This alterity is even the condition of Presence, of presentation and therefore of *Vorstellung* in general, before all of the associations which may be produced" (VP 73; trans. 65 modified). As opposed to Deleuze, who criticizes this misestimation of repetition as a weakness in the philosophy of representation, which by implication could be amended or improved by a more rigorous analysis, Derrida here seems to say: that's right, that's how it is. There is an original difference at work in any act of representation, even in the instant of perception, as Husserl, perhaps unintentionally, has shown. This original difference Derrida calls the *trace*.

Derrida identifies this *trace* as the working of *différance* in a terminology shift that is of great importance: "The *trace* in the universal sense is a possibility which must not only inhabit the pure actuality of the now, but constitute that actuality by the same movement of *différance* it introduces therein. Such a trace is, if one can keep this language and erase it [*le raturer*] at the same time, more 'originary' than the phenomenological 'originarity' itself" (VP 75; trans. 67 modified; my italics). Following closely what he says here, we can identify the "movement of *différance*" as a preconceptual or nonconceptual moment in the constitution of any thought or perception. As a nonconceptual movement, this *différance* cannot really be thought in the context of the philosophical conversation as we know it. Thus Derrida introduces the language "difficulties," the action of *raturer* that in the *Grammatology* will be the *sous rature* (or continuing to use a word which the force of analysis has shown to be outworn or inadequate, but cannot be stated otherwise within a certain language of investigation), a strain in language that reflects the inability to think language outside of language.

Différance is not merely an affair of language (that is, it is neither simply a pun, nor restricted to the sphere of language). As Derrida was clear to outline at the outset of his study of Husserl's theory of expression, a view of language is also a view of the subject. What happens to the transcendental subject in Derrida's analysis? It is also affected, indeed comes about, through a "movement of *différance.*" Derrida states: "Self-affectivity [*L'auto-affection*] as an operation of the voice supposed that a pure difference came to divide the presence-to-self. It is in this pure difference that the possibility takes hold of everything we believe it possible to exclude from self-affectivity: space, the outside, the world, the body, etc. As soon as we admit that self-affectivity is the condition of presence-to-self, no transcendental reduction is possible. But we must make our way through it in order to grasp again difference as closely as possible: not its identity, nor its purity, nor its origin. It has none of these. *But the movement of différance*" (VP 92; trans. 82 modified; my italics). Derrida seems not to reject the "transcendental reduction" of Husserl, even seeming to claim that we must follow it out to get close to difference, or what difference might mean. At the same time he clearly places the philosophy of self-understanding as "hearing-oneself-speak" in radical question.[11] Driving the wedge into the Husserlian constitution of the subject, as an example of the metaphysics of presence, with the unheard little "a" of *différance,* Derrida opens speech and writing up for a still more radical critique.

Derrida begins with the unheard little "a" of *différance* in his 1968 lecture of that title (M 1–29; trans. 1–27). The original difference between perception and retention, between experience and the meaning the transcendental subject makes of that experience (that he showed with respect to Husserl's theory of expression), is the nonconceptual *trace* that underlies meaning and perception. And if he discovered this *différance* in an investigation of language, this is because (in a founding, not merely a causal way) language, or writing, is already this *trace.* The little "a" in *différance* gives the word a productive or verbal force, recalling more forcefully the two senses of the verb *différer:* (1) "to temporize" (*"temporiser"*) and (2) "not to be identical, to be other," (*"ne pas être identique, être autre"*) or "spacing" (*"espacement"*) (M 8; trans. 8). This latter would seem to lead, he says, to the Heideggerian questioning of ontological difference; but he also says he will "delay" his response to this (M 10; trans. 10). By this little detour into the word and its spelling, Derrida seems to be proposing an *example* (in the appearance of the written word itself) rather than a *concept* (its meaning).

The effect of the unheard difference in the written word is the effect of the *trace* or *writing* in general: which, he says: "I propose to call arche-writing, arche-trace or difference. This latter (is) (at the same time) spacing (and) temporization" (M 14; trans. 13 modified). It will take the more elaborate working out of the *Grammatology* to make the case for the *trace* as "writing" (which I will examine shortly). In this brief essay, Derrida wants to investigate some of the consequences for thinking of this double *trace*, in part because his appointment with Heidegger yet awaits him.

Language is based on the pure play of difference, according to Saussure (M 11; trans. 11). Yet Saussure's conception of difference is really simple opposition, as Deleuze argues. This difference found in language (spoken language, or *langue*) can be more radically thought by the *trace* in language (written language, or Derrida's expanded sense of *écriture*). Since philosophy is conceived of as *logic* (*logos*), these same constitutive oppositions can be shown to organize philosophical discourse as well. As Derrida states in the context of a discussion of Nietzsche: "This does not exclude that within the same logic, within logic itself, philosophy lives *in* and *by différance*, blinding itself thereby to the same that is not the identical. The same is precisely *différance* (with an *a*) as the means of access, detoured and equivocal, of one different to the other, of one term of opposition to another" (M 18; trans. 17 modified). And if this were as far as *différance* were taken—as the effect of "writing" in the philosophical discourse—we would not be that far from Heidegger's philosophy of the Same, or Deleuze's nonconceptual or productive difference. This is why the double turn, both "spacing" *and* "temporization," is needed, and that necessitates an investigation of the non-Kantian working of time that Derrida finds in the writings of Freud.[12]

In a brilliant, compact reading of Freud, and especially in *Beyond the Pleasure Principle*, Derrida finds support for the workings of *différance* in both senses, as "spacing" (*Spur* or *trace*) and "temporization" (*Aufschub* or *détour*). This working of *différance* as both *trace* and *détour* Freud called the unconscious: "A certain alterity—to which Freud gives the metaphysical name of the unconscious. . . . This radical alterity in relation to any possible mode of presence is marked by the irreducible effects of after-the-fact, of delay [d'après-coup, de retardement]" (M 21; trans. 20–21 modified). This "*structure de retardement (Nachträchligkeit)*" is the delay Freud identifies in the workings of the unconscious, and which he also describes in terms of the "mystic writing pad" (cf. Derrida, "Freud et la scène de l'écriture," ED 293–340; WD 196–231). Like the difference between *Vorstellung* and *presence*, the delay between retention and originary perception, or retention as originary perception and meaning in Husserl, the delay Derrida finds here in Freud's description of the workings of the unconscious, radically undermines the self-consistency of the subject. As Derrida states: "With the alterity of the 'unconscious,' we are concerned not with modified horizons of the present—whether past or still to come—but with *a 'past' which was never present* [my italics] and never will be, of which the 'future' [*l'a-venir'* or 'still-to-come'] will never be the *production* or reproduction in the form of presence. The concept of trace is therefore incommensurable with that of retention, of the becoming-past of what was present. One cannot think the trace—and therefore *différance*—starting from the present, or of the presence of the present" (M 22; trans. 21 modified). This is a strong statement of Derrida's position on the effect of the *trace* as an undermining of the metaphysics of presence.[13] The movement of *différance* or the *trace* picks up powerful momentum from this analysis of the effects of the unconscious.

With this momentum, Derrida is prepared to return to his (delayed) encounter with Heidegger's questioning of the ontological difference. At no point is it a question of offering a "critique" of Heidegger's meditations. Rather, the question of the difference between Being and beings shows the structure of forgetting and concealment (as analyzed above). Referring specifically to Heidegger's essay, "The Anaximander Fragment," Derrida finds that the ontological difference is described as a forgetting or concealment of difference. This Derrida redefines as the *trace* of *différance*, leading to the following paradox: "The paradox of such a structure is, in the language of metaphysics, this inversion of the metaphysical concept which produces the following effect: the present becomes the sign of a sign, the trace of a trace. It is no longer that which in the final instance every return returns to. It becomes a function in a generalized structure of return. *It is the trace of a trace and the effacement of the trace*" (M 25; trans. 24 modified; my italics). Heidegger's project leads him to hope (*"l'espérance heideggerrienne"*) in a sole or "unique word" (*das einzige Wort*), which Derrida implies is a certain nostalgia of presence. The structure of the sign as "trace of a trace" and as "the effacing of the trace" is a central step in Derrida's analysis, one that he carries through more extensively in the *Grammatology*.

Derrida's project in the *Grammatology* [G] is nothing less than a "deconstruction" of the entire Western metaphysics of presence, a deconstruction accomplished through the reversal of the traditional privileging of speech over writing. Derrida demonstrates that the *archi-écriture* uncovered by the *trace* or *différance* is the nonoriginal "originary" movement that allows for and enables all forms of intersubjective contact, including writing, thinking, and philosophy as well as every human form of economic, religious, or political system. Indeed, once there is an interpersonal power structure of any sort, writing is "always already" at work. The profound implications of such a stance have continued to occupy Derrida in his subsequent work, not the least of these being the ethical ramifications such a stance implies.[14] Here I will maintain the rather limited focus on difference already established by what has preceded in this analysis, linking up with the investigation of the Heideggerian questioning of ontological difference, using it as an Ariadne's thread or *fil conducteur* through the labyrinth.

Right at the outset of the *Grammatology*, Derrida rejoins the debate with Heidegger and the question of the onto-theological difference. In the philosophy of the *logos*, which Derrida claims Heidegger does not escape, there must be a "transcendental signified" in order to establish a fundamental difference between signifier and signified: "There has to be a transcendental signified for the difference between signifier and signified to be somewhere absolute and irreducible" (G 33; trans. 20). The transcendental signified would be another term for the "unique word" (*das einzige Wort*) which Derrida implies is a sign of a certain nostalgia for presence (as above). Derrida argues further on, in Heidegger's own terms, that, if the progressive forgetting of Being is not purely historical, but can only be thought in terms of the history of Being itself, then the action of the word (*logos*) or signifier must take a certain priority: "Heidegger's insistence on noting that being is produced as history only through the logos, and is nothing outside of it, the difference between Being and beings—all this clearly indicates that fundamentally nothing escapes the movement of the signifier and that, in the last instance, the difference between signified and signifier *is* nothing" (G 36; trans. 22–23; italics in the original). If the history of Being is the progressive forgetting of the difference between Being and beings, this is because, according to Derrida, there is already a progressive effacement of the difference or *trace* that produces the sign or word. This then is *différance* and must come "first": "*Différance* by itself would be more 'originary,' but one would no longer be able to call it 'origin' or 'ground,' those notions belonging essentially to the history of onto-theology, to the system functioning as the effacing of difference" (G 38; trans. 23). Statements like this are one reason why the *Grammatology* can be such a disturbing work. The ground of Being, traced through in the language of Heidegger, the philosopher who did the most to discover it, simply seems to open up in an endless regress of "prior" *différance.*

The main part of the first half of the work takes the philosophical issue of onto-theology and works it back through the tradition of thinking about language. As with *Speech and Phenomena*, the layer of language is shown to be anything but ancillary, or perhaps more accurately, of crucial importance because ancillary. If Derrida used the speech/language wedge to open up the Husserlian phenomenology of the subject's constitution, he here uses the Husserlian phenomenology to break apart the implicit metaphysics of Saussurian linguistics. Having dismissed the ordinary concept of "experience" (G 89; trans. 60; see note 9), he here focuses on the theory of how language represents that experience—and finds it lacking. Before any difference can appear between experience and its representation, there must already be the trace: "*The (pure) trace is differance*" ("*La trace (pure) est la différance,*" G 92; trans. 62; italics in the original). *Différance* in this sense is the larger movement of "writing" that Derrida's work seeks to explore. "Writing" thus precedes speech or even the customary distinctions between the two: "If language were not already, in that sense, a writing, no derived 'notation' would be possible; and the classical problem of relationships between speech and writing could not arise" (G 92; trans. 63). In a deft move, Derrida shows that the signifier/signified relationship is derived from a quasi-naive reading of Husserlian phenomenology and the *hylè/morphè* distinction. Thus perception is likewise a *trace*, and subject to "writing": "The unheard difference between the appearing and the appearance [*l'apparaissant et l'apparaître*] (between the 'world' and 'lived experience') is the condition of all other differences, of all other traces, and *it is already a trace*" (G 95; trans. 65; italics in the original). The circle is closed, but the gap in the traditional concept of the subject has widened.

Writing in the larger sense that Derrida develops in the *Grammatology* refers to the inscription of the subject within preexisting laws, language, social customs, religion, and much more. Thus when he

turns to his unsparing examination of Lévi-Strauss's Rousseauist tendencies in a chapter called "The Violence of the Letter," Derrida is
only secondarily interested in the "violence" done by the ethnologist
to the "innocent" indigenous culture he studies. The whole question
becomes, rather: "What links writing to violence?" ("Or qu'est-ce qui
lie l'écriture à la violence?" G 149; trans. 101). The movement of *différance* by which the *trace* is endlessly effaced is in its "positive" sense
the institution of difference in a network of power relations. The "innocent" culture (Rousseau) that would correspond to the idea of a
"society without writing" simply does not exist. As Derrida says: "If
writing is no longer understood in the narrow sense of linear and
phonetic notation, it should be possible to say that all societies capable
of producing, that is to say obliterating, their proper names, and of
bringing classificatory difference into play, practice writing in general.
No reality or concept would therefore correspond to the expression
'society without writing'" (G 161; trans. 109). The important point that
is raised is one that comes in almost obliquely into Derrida's text. He
asks (and there is no temptation to write "in all innocence"): "If it is
true, as I in fact believe, that *writing cannot be thought outside of the
horizon of intersubjective violence,* is there anything, even science,
that radically escapes it?" (G 185; trans. 127; my italics). Not only is
Lévi-Strauss not guilty of violating an innocent people's purity by showing them writing, their society was violent before he arrived. And the
further question that is raised here (the phrase "cannot be thought
outside of the horizon" carrying the full weight of the phenomenological tradition), whether *writing* is ever separable from *intersubjective
violence,* shows the ethical force of Derrida's thinking. As my discussion in the final two chapters follows this out more fully, if there is
such a thing as an ethics of deconstruction, Derrida's question here
points to a significant way to think—or write—it.

Whatever else it is, *Glas* is certainly a project of writing.[15] The
"writerly" aspect is highlighted by the celebrated disposition of the
text on the page, with two columns referring generally to Hegel (left)
and Genet (right), with extended quotations, mimicking, textual in-
serts or "tattoos," and even made-up dialogues between long-dead philosophers of the tradition (241a ff.; 216a ff.). The razzle-dazzle (*glas,
Klang,* whatever) of the text has largely been responsible for shifting
attention towards the play of language and words (for all their usefulness, the English translation and accompanying *Glossary* take this to

an extreme) and away from the important ethical dimension in Derrida's work this text demonstrates. *Différance* as such is not so much in evidence in this text, but this is because Derrida's concerns have shifted from the *trace* (endlessly becoming unmotivated of the sign) through *différance* to the *remainder* (*le reste*), the unassimilable difference, or what remains, resisting knowledge and interpretation.

The subtitle to *Glas, What remains of absolute knowledge?* (*Que reste-il du savoir absolu?*), implies a certain attempt to reclaim Hegel's philosophical project for present day uses. The *remains* (*reste*) that is a verb here appears more often in the text as a noun and indicates the unassimilable difference between Hegel's (lost) intentions in writing his text and what we can make of it today. Also, perhaps even more important, the *remainder* is the "other," the different one, "the case of Genet" ("le cas Genet," 37b; 29b), that resists the universalizing aspect of any philosophical system, but especially Hegel's, in his analysis of love, sexual difference, and the family. Like *différance*, the *remainder* is not a concept, cannot even be thought in the conceptual logic, and yet is what resists the famous *Aufhebung* of Hegel: "To sum up, a remainder that would not be without being nothing: a remainder which isn't" ("En somme un reste qui ne soit pas sans être un néant: un reste qui ne soit," 53a; trans. 43a modified). This is an instance when the two columns appear to look at each other: "the infinite exchange of two columns which gaze backwards at each other [l'échange infini de deux colonnes qui se regardent à l'envers]" (53b; trans. 43b modified). The two columns intertwining, "X, almost perfect chiasmus [X, chiasme presque parfait]" (53b; trans. 43b modified), are like the experiences of looking at a painting that Genet describes in "What Remains of a Rembrandt [Ce qui reste d'un Rembrandt]". Some issues that Derrida locates in Genet's texts are transvestism, play of true and false in sexual and textual terms, the "case" of one who even in his text does not sign or identify himself and yet is all his characters. These issues are precisely those which would seem to offer maximum resistance to the Hegelian *Aufhebung*; from the Genet side, "Remains to be seen (or known) [Reste à savoir]" (55b; trans. 45b modified).

Derrida offers an extended reading of Hegel on the family and on sexual difference itself. Concerning Hegel's treatment of sexual difference, Derrida claims: "Copulation relieves the difference: the *Aufhebung* is very precisely the relation of copulation and sexual difference" (127a; 111a). The male in Hegel's analysis represents the principle of differ-

ence, the female indifference. Difference writ large, originating difference, the difference that at once is and calls for the *Aufhebung*, is the
opposition between the male and female. This, then, is the place of
sexual intercourse within the family as it represents the move in philosophy to a philosophy of ethics, what Hegel terms *Sittlichkeit* (often
translated as "social morality"). While this rich series of meditations is
going on in the one column, the "case" of Genet seems to resist assimilation into the Hegelian model of the family. Abandoned by his mother
at an early age, Genet entered first into the home of a foster family,
then a center for juvenile delinquents, and, following a marginal criminal career, into jail (almost) for life. What do we have here that would
confirm or disconfirm the Hegelian model? *"Remains—the mother
[Reste—la mère]"* (132b; 115b). All of this is nearly inextricable from
parallel meditations on law and the death penalty (Hegel), the glory of
the criminal Harcamone sentenced to die (Genet), castration, relating
back to decapitation (both sides), fetishism (both sides), crime in general, and intersubjective violence.

In my view, *Glas* is at least in part the extension of the line of
thinking suggested obliquely in the *Grammatology* on the horizon for
writing, or *différance*, as intersubjective violence. The classical philosopher Hegel would see difference, even ultimate determining difference, as a moment in the movement towards absolute knowledge.
Derrida's move is not to dismiss the project of absolute knowledge, but
to insist on the *remainder (reste)* that blocks the ideality of the philosopher's expression. Difference as writing—writing as intersubjective
violence—demonstrates that our human culture is founded on difference, and is thus inevitably violent, and can never finally be assimi-
lated to a purely conceptual model of human existence. In the *Grammatology*, Derrida showed that difference is "always already"; in *Glas*
he shows why we can't shake it: "The bloody detachment is also—
repetition—delegation, mandate, delay, relay. Adherence. The detached
remains stuck by that, by the glue of differance, by the a. The a of gl
agglutinates the detached differences. The scaffold of the A is gluey [Le
détachement sanglant est aussi—répétition—délégation, mandat, dé-
lai, relais. Adhérence. Le détaché reste collé par là, par la glu de la
différance, par l'a. L'a de gl agglutine les différences détachés. L'échafaud de l'A est gluant]" (188b; trans. 167b modified). We might compare
this with the culmination to a long series of meditations on Hegel's
interpretations of *Antigone* and *Oedipus*: "The scene of the crime be-

ing opened between two laws (singularity/universality, woman/man), being read on two panels, there is no murder that is not the (ethical) effect of sexual opposition. Every crime is a sexual and familial operation [La scène du crime s'ouvrant entre deux lois (singularité/universalité, femme/homme), se lisant sur ses deux tableaux, il n'est pas de meurtre qui ne soit l'effet (éthique) de l'opposition sexuelle. Tout crime est une opération sexuelle et familiale]" (195a; trans. 173a modified). Sexual difference, crime, specifically murder—these are the subjects of both sides of the text. How can knowledge claim to exercise a sovereign claim over what we *know* life to be? *Glas* insists on the irreducible difference, the *remainder* (*reste*) that blocks any knowledge from being absolute, at the same time as following the philosophy of law to its most crucial foundations. The resulting series of reflections shows that difference is ultimately not entirely knowable, but that we must act and think nonetheless in the face of the deepest ethical challenge it presents us.

Difference in the philosophy of Heidegger is at the very least a strong incitement to continued thinking of crucial issues of language, philosophy, and society in the works of Deleuze and Derrida. Whereas Deleuze in *Différence et répétition* remains within a certain post-Kantian framework while pointing to the necessary limitations of such a framework, Derrida, in his works from the sixties and early seventies, radicalizes difference through his thinking on *différance.* Viewed from the standpoint of the ethics of deconstruction, *Glas* stands as a pivotal work, both exploring the repercussions of the expanded sense of "writing" as "intersubjective violence" and introducing different textual strategies for interrogating the philosophical tradition. I return to a discussion of *Glas* in chapter 6's analysis of deconstruction's "impossible" ethics; but the question of intersubjective violence and the position of the ethical subject founded on resistance to such violence require an investigation into the ethical thinking of Emmanuel Levinas and Julia Kristeva.

Chapter Four

Levinas and the Ethics of Exteriority

The philosophy of Emmanuel Levinas serves to point a way beyond the apparent impasses brought about by the Lacanian and deconstructive theories of the subject. Levinas's view of *exteriority* stems from a deep engagement with the phenomenological inquiries into the constitution of the subject as well as the religious tradition of Judaism, especially in its ethical aspect.[1] *Exteriority* in Levinas's thinking represents the other-directed thrust of human existence, especially in the ethical instance that is both a response to the call of the other and the need to resist intersubjective violence. The challenge and vitality of Levinas's thought is clear in the range of response to his ideas that I will be exploring by writers as diverse as Derrida, Maurice Blanchot, Jean-François Lyotard, and Luce Irigaray. The radical *exteriority* Levinas proposes—as coming in some important sense *before* the institution of writing and difference—bears on many of the important debates in current theory and criticism. Levinas's view that *teaching* is exteriority as openness, for example, presents an ethical model for interpretive practice in the institutional framework. Moreover, the work of writers such as Irigaray shows how feminist theory has dynamically reappropriated some of the ideas on sexual difference implied by Levinas's *exteriority*.[2]

In Levinas's 1961 study, *Totality and Infinity: An Essay on Exteriority*, exteriority figures as a mediating term between the two large conceptual markers of the main title. In Levinas's initial description of exteriority, the face of the other and *the remainder* (*reste*) are both present in the conception. He states: "We can proceed from the experience of totality back to a situation where totality breaks up, a situation that conditions the totality itself. *Such a situation is the flash [éclat] of exteriority or of transcendence in the face of the other. The rigorously developed concept of this transcendence is expressed by the term infinity"* (TI xiii; trans. 24–25 modified; my italics). As a mediating term, exteriority derives from a "transcendent experience," presumably one in which the individual subject feels his or her limits to be exceeded. This transcendence in the philosophy of Merleau-Ponty results from the position of the subject in the act of perception. The transcendent experience in Levinas's philosophy is the face of the other. Levinas terms this transcendence "infinity" because it surpasses the bounds of conceptual thought, what can be thought: "In the idea of infinity is thought what remains always exterior to thinking" (TI xiii; trans. 25 modified). Exteriority, even in this initial juncture of defining terms, must be seen both as physically exterior to the subject—the face of the other—and as metaphorical—what exceeds thought.

Of course the philosophical tradition has always termed the latter experience of transcendence "metaphysics," a term that Levinas adopts readily, though not without some problems for his analysis. A respect for exteriority, in Levinas's metaphysical thinking, is what constitutes truth: "The aspiration to radical exteriority, thus called metaphysical, the respect for this metaphysical exteriority which, above all, we must 'let be'—constitutes truth" (TI xvii; trans. 29). What quickly becomes apparent is that, for Levinas, metaphysics is not an abstract science, but what allows for ethical response. As he says: "The traditional opposition between theory and practice will disappear before the metaphysical transcendence by which a relation with the absolutely other, or truth, is established, and of which ethics is the royal road" (TI xvii; trans. 29). From the beginning to the end of this work, Levinas never stops insisting that morality is the "first philosophy." This is the meaning of his connection between ethics and exteriority: "Ethics, beyond vision and certitude, designates the structure of exteriority as such. Morality is not a branch of philosophy, but the first philosophy" (TI 281; trans. 304 modified). In this way, Levinas reorients philosophical priorities, since Aristotle had called ontology the "first philosophy." Ethics derives from the structure of exteriority because the first step to interrelation (and thus the basis for subjectivity) is the call of the other, the demand placed before us by the other's face.

The truth of experience for Levinas is always encountered in an orientation of the subject toward the other. One of the key terms for this thinking is, not surprisingly, desire. In language that recalls (or anticipates) Lacan, Levinas says: "Infinity is not an 'object' of knowledge . . . but is the desirable, that which arouses Desire, i.e. what is approachable through a thinking which at each instant *thinks more than can be thought* [pense plus qu'elle ne pense]. Infinity is not thereby an immense object, exceeding the horizons of the gaze. It is Desire that measures the infinity of the infinite, for it is a measure through the very impossibility of measure. The boundless [*démesure*] measured by Desire is the face" (TI 33; trans. 62 modified; italics in the original). Among the many possible entries into this passage, we might begin with the italicized phrase, especially its use of the "*ne explétif*" so prized by Lacan.[3] Lacan returns insistently to the solitary "*ne*" because of the split it institutes between the subject of the thought and the subject of enunciation, exactly its role here, indicating on the level of content a surpassing of the subject in what "is more than what can be thought." Desire in Levinas's thought, as in Lacan's, is a motive force, driving the subject at the same time as orienting it outside itself.[4] This is the reason infinity is not an "object," exceeding rational thought as it exceeds the bounds of the subject.

The face, or *visage*, is another key term in the development of exteriority as traced so far. Tied to the ethics of exteriority, the face of the other calls to the subject.[5] This is because, for Levinas, the face is never mute, but always expressive: "The face is a living presence; it is expression" (TI 37; trans. 66). This expression is language, discourse, communication. Like desire, the notion of the face is always relational, calling the subject out of its isolation, or inwardness, and into the sphere of the community. The face in Levinas's thought precedes law, yet leads to his concept of justice: "Metaphysics or transcendence is recognized in the work of the intellect that aspires to the exteriority which is Desire. But the Desire for exteriority has appeared to us to stem, not from objective knowledge, but from Discourse, which in turn presents itself as justice, in the rightness of the welcome extended to the face" (TI 54; trans. 82 modified). The face of the other calls to the subject, the subject whose openness to the outside is desire. Before the law that would regulate this encounter, the sense of justice is created by the subject's openness to the other.

Another word for this openness to the other, or aspiration toward exteriority, in Levinas's terms, is *enseignement*, or teaching. Language by its very structure implicates the community in a way that Derrida, for example, has explored. Levinas's theory of teaching, however, may point a way for us to resist the intersubjective violence Derrida sees as the inevitable horizon for language as writing. Being is discourse because it is first of all active and relational. Levinas states: "The transitivity of teaching, and not the interiority of reminiscence, manifests being. Society is the place of truth" (TI 74; trans. 101 modified). In a line of thinking that could equally well be applied to the production of the text, Levinas goes on to say that teaching is not the representation to another of truth, but the production itself of that truth: "Teaching signifies the whole infinity of exteriority. And the whole infinity of exteriority is not first produced, to then teach—teaching is its very production. The first teaching teaches this very height which even equals its exteriority, ethics" (TI 146; trans. 171 modified). Just as there are other philosophies, but only one "first philosophy"—and for Levinas this is morality—so the primary goal of teaching, the highest to which it may aspire, is ethics.

Exteriority as face (*visage*) and as teaching (*l'enseignement*) both point to the necessary involvement of the subject in language. Language arises from difference and institutes ethics: "Absolute difference . . . is established only by language" (TI 168; trans. 195). Language in so doing breaks down the isolation and interiority of the subject: "*The being of signification consists in subjecting to question in an ethical relation constitutive freedom itself*" (TI 181; trans. 206 modified; italics in the original). Language in Levinas's thinking is both the source and possibility of exteriority. His theory of language itself may be criticized for its lack of complexity (the sign renders the reference exterior to the subject in the sense of Frege's *Bedeutung*, TI 184; trans. 209). But the next step into violence and ethics radicalizes phenomenology and anticipates what Derrida has shown to be the horizon for deconstruction. Discourse, before leading to the possibility for abstract thought, engages the human subject in the ethical situation of violence and the first ethical command to resist such violence. As Levinas states: "Discourse conditions thinking, since the first sign of intelligence is not a concept, but an intelligence whose inviolable exteriority the face states in uttering the 'you shall not commit murder.' The essence of discourse is ethics. By announcing this thesis, we refuse idealism" (TI 184; trans. 216 modified). This central passage clearly refutes the entire idealist tradition instituted by Descartes and entailing necessarily the famous "problem of others." Discourse is not first a means by which the subject constitutes itself in the *cogito*, according to Levinas, but the source and necessity of relation with the other. This is not to say, as Derrida does—mistakenly, I believe—that Levinas's philosophy is "empiricist" (ED 224; WD 151–52).

The clearest reason why Levinas cannot be classed as an empiricist is that, finally, the guarantor of exteriority, in his sense, is God. The "Je/tu" relation implied in the above citation, which Levinas derives complexly from Martin Buber (TI 40ff.; trans. 68ff.), means primarily that God intervenes in the relation of intersubjective violence *before* the formulation of the Law. According to Levinas, one must first simply give in to this call from the other: "Being is exteriority: the very exercise of its being consists in exteriority, and no thinking could better obey being than by allowing itself to be dominated by this exteriority" (TI 266; trans. 290 modified). Clearly the interrelational structure that Levinas evokes is complex and difficult to reduce to such schemata as idealism vs. empiricism. His thinking on exteriority arises out of a specific religious tradition in complex interaction with phenomenological currents. The ethical position his thought posits as primary and irreducible places in question both the traditional interior/exterior distinction and the poststructuralist dogma of language as law.

Derrida's early essay on the thought of Levinas, "Violence and Metaphysics" (ED 116–228; WD 79–153), is one of his most rigorously structured pieces, indicating a profound respect for Levinas's positions at the same time as moving to establish some of the key tenets of Derrida's own philosophy. In his examination of Levinas's thought on exteriority, Derrida points to the nonspatial aspect of exteriority, that is, exteriority not as it is normally understood, as revealing the difference between philosophical language and everyday use of language (ED 165–69; WD 112–15). This may be seen as Derrida's way of commending Levinas's practice before subjecting it to an intense scrutiny. This scrutiny takes the primary form of using the philosophies of Husserl and Heidegger back against Levinas's notion of the subject. In the view Derrida advances in this essay, Levinas misestimates Husserl's and Heidegger's thinking on the constitution of the subject and language, attributing an intersubjective violence, or totalitarianism, to their thinking on the subject's relation to others. In turn, this causes Levinas to ignore or misunderstand the "pre-ethical violence" that precedes even the constitution of the subject (ED 184, 188; WD 125, 128). This double turn is necessary so that Derrida's own philosophy of intersubjective violence as the horizon for "writing" can emerge with clearer distinction.

Derrida places himself in the philosophical position of shoring up key moves made by Husserl and Heidegger, so he can subsequently open up his own breach in Levinas's philosophy of the subject. Husserl's theory of the self's relation to the other operates by means of an "analogical appresentation" of the other's ego to one's own. That is to say, I represent the other to myself by analogy: he/she has a subjectivity similar to my own that allows me to approximate his/her experience through reference to my own experience and thereby gain understanding of the other's subjectivity. This analogical appresentation does *not* do violence to the other's ego, Derrida claims, but rather respects the other's alterity (ED 182; WD 124). The refusal to acknowledge the validity of analogical appresentation, according to Derrida, undermines Levinas's whole theory of the other. As Derrida says: "Levinas *in fact* speaks of the infinitely other, but by refusing to acknowledge an intentional modification of the ego—which would be a violent and totalitarian act for him—he deprives himself of the very foundation and the possibility of his own language" (ED 183; WD 125). This is an extremely startling statement, in that Derrida seems to be defending the intentional quality of the ego as the basis for language and subjectivity. At the risk of seeming to deconstruct the discourse of deconstruction, I would pose the question of whether this stance would hold up to the philosophy of the *remainder (reste)* developed in *Glas*, as discussed in the previous chapter. My view is that Derrida's later ethical philosophy, which I examine in my final two chapters, in fact brings him much closer to Levinas's ethics of exteriority, which in turn offers Derrida a means of interrogating the status of the ethical subject of discourse.[6]

Derrida's goal in posing the question of the subject in this way is to open up the possibility of what he calls "a pre-ethical violence" (ED 184; WD 125). This violence is, of course, the institution of "writing" that the *Grammatology* defines in terms of "the horizon of intersubjective violence" (G 185; trans. 127). In effect, then, Derrida defends Husserl from Levinas's charge that analogical appresentation does violence to the other, so that Derrida can discover intersubjective violence at an ontologically prior stage. As he states: "There is a transcendental and pre-ethical violence, a dissymmetry (in general), of which the *arche* is the same and which allows finally a reverse dissymmetry, the ethical non-violence of which Levinas speaks" (ED 188; WD 128 [trans. modified]). The language of the same, and of radical difference, is used here back against Levinas. "The infinitely other" of Levinas is only guaranteed by the face of the other as God, and thus, the same. In a footnote, Derrida claims Hegel's philosophy points more clearly to a way of respecting and preserving difference: "Alterity, difference, and time are not *suppressed* but *retained* by absolute knowledge in the form of the *Aufhebung*" (ED 190; WD 316 n47). Once again, it is inconceivable to me that the Derrida of *Glas* could write this sentence, in that the "absolute knowledge," here presented as the determining instance, is subjected to radical questioning from exactly the standpoint of a deconstructive ethics.

Saving Husserl from Levinas, using Hegel's *Aufhebung* to refute Levinas's notion of difference as "the absolutely other," Derrida even defends Heidegger from Levinas's devastating critique concerning Heidegger's alleged totalitarianism and agrarian sedentarism (ED 213ff.; WD 144ff.). Derrida's defense of Heidegger is once again motivated by a desire to use Heidegger's philosophy to underpin the notion of pre-ethical violence. In the philosophy of concealment and forgetting of Being, Heidegger recognizes, says Derrida, that the progressive unveiling of Being requires violence: "This signifies first off that being is history, that it dissimulates itself in its production and presents itself originarily as violence in thinking in order to be spoken and to appear" (ED 218; WD 147 [trans. modified]). This would seem to me to lead to the charge, not that Levinas is an empiricist, but rather that he is an essentialist. In fact, essentialism is the payoff to Derrida's use of Heidegger back against Levinas. Derrida states: "Thus, in its highest non-violent exigency, denouncing the passage by means of being and the moment of the concept, the thought of Levinas not only would propose, as we were saying before, *an ethics without law but also a language without statement*" (ED 219; WD 147 [trans. modified]; my italics). As my further analysis will attempt to show, "an ethics without law" and "a language without statement" are in fact the same charge, law and language being equated at this historical (poststructuralist) moment of criticism. An example of this is Lacan's Symbolic realm of language, guaranteed by the Law of the Father, or *le nom du père*, which I discuss below.

Maurice Blanchot's long study, *L'Entretien infini* (*The Infinite Conversation*, 1969), explores some of the same arguments concerning exteriority, writing, and the law in discussing the philosophy of Levinas. One essay, "Knowledge of the Unknown" (EI 70–83), presents an extended, respectful discussion of *Totality and Infinity*, indicating as well an awareness of Derrida's essay on Levinas (EI 80n). Throughout *L'Entretien infini* Blanchot's use of the term *exteriority* seems informed by Levinas's work. Blanchot is primarily interested in the relation between exteriority and writing, ultimately establishing a dialectic between exteriority as law and exteriority as writing. Blanchot, however, is absolutely uninterested in the term "ethics"; as he says, "I only find in this word derived meanings" (EI 89). There is a general concurrence in this work with Derrida's views that law and language are inconceivable separately and that Levinas's thinking on exteriority needs to be corrected by reasserting the primacy of the law.

Writing for Blanchot, as discourse or the sign for Levinas, uncovers a structure of exteriority. This for Blanchot is the "attraction" of writing: "The attraction of (pure) exteriority—the place where, the outside 'preceding' any interior, writing does not place itself in the manner of a spiritual or ideal presence inscribing itself afterwards and giving way afterwards to a trace, trace or sedimentary deposit which will permit a following to its trace, i.e. to restore it, starting with this mark as lack, in its ideal presence or its ideality, its plenitude, its integrity of presence" (EI 625). We see here the double exteriority that Levinas proposes, both spatial and metaphorical. The advance in the thinking of Blanchot is over the rather too simplistic notion of sign as external reference, moving toward a Derridean conception of writing as trace. The clear thrust here is to eliminate the notion of writing as an external aid to the recording of interior states, such interior states then being recoverable through following the trace back to the original thought. Rather, writing as exteriority defeats such an idealism of the subject, with all of the metaphysical trappings such a model implies.

Blanchot takes this thinking on writing and exteriority and introduces the related notions of the book and the law. When writing becomes a book, then the exteriority it represents becomes an exteriority of the law: "The exteriority of writing, ranging and stratifying itself in the book, becomes exteriority as law" (EI 632). This statement shows just how far Blanchot has moved from the concept of exteriority proposed by Levinas. For Levinas, exteriority as the face of the other and the ethical injunction to nonviolence precedes establishment of the law. For Blanchot, (pure) exteriority integrates itself into the Book, under the sign of the law, bringing knowledge and desire into play. For Blanchot's analysis, such a progression is portrayed as inevitable, since the act of writing is necessarily produced under the auspices of the law: "In other words, one cannot move backwards from exteriority as law to exteriority as writing. The law is the summit, there is no other. Writing remains outside arbitration between high and low" (EI 626). Though this aspect of Blanchot's thinking is extremely rich, it also shows, to my mind, the free-floating quality of an exteriority not tied to an ethical dimension. The role of the ethical subject and the community in the writing project would be a difficult question to resolve.

The pure exteriority of Blanchot, an effect of writing in relation to the law, leads, in my reading, to a free-floating, difficult-to-resolve idea of exteriority that largely ignores the ethical dimension insisted on by Levinas. Jacques Lacan's theory of the subject as constituted in and through the specular relation to the Other presents a different model of pure exteriority. Although Lacan's theory presents language as operating under the *Nom du père*, Law [*lit.* Name] of the Father, his discussion of exteriority may help to anchor the discussion more firmly in the ethical realm. Lacan's statements on exteriority refer to the necessary exteriorization of the subject's image so that it may return in a recognizable form. He describes the structure: "In other words the privilege of the *moi* in relation to things needs to be sought elsewhere than in that false recurrence to infinity which constitutes the mirage of consciousness, and which despite its perfect inanity still intoxicates those who work on thinking until they see in it a *supposed progress of interiority,* while it is rather in a topological phenomenon the distribution of which in nature is as sporadic as the *dispositions of pure exteriority* which condition it, even if it is man who has contributed to spreading them with an immoderate frequency" (E 424; my translation and italics). In a perceptive insight, Mark Taylor links the pure exteriority invoked here to Lacan's theory of the Real (A 94). Lacan's Real as exteriority is not simply the world exterior to the subject. From the context of this statement it is clear that the exteriority described is structured by the mirror-stage principle of image identification. The phenomena so rare in nature to which Lacan refers and which humans have caused to proliferate are, it would seem, mirrors. Consciousness is a mere "mirage" if the possibility of reflection is attributed to the "presumed progress of interiority." Rather than conscious reflection, says Lacan, we ought to turn our attention to exterior phenomena of reflection, discovering therein the true dimension of exteriority as the alienating function of the ego's necessary self-reflective tendencies.

Lacan returns, in his seminar on the ethics of psychoanalysis (*Séminaire VII: L'Éthique de la psychanalyse*), to an extensive working out of this structure of exteriority he terms "the Real." With primary reference to Aristotle's, Kant's, and Freud's thinking on ethics, the seminar is Lacan's fundamental treatment of the question of ethics in the analytic setting, given the dimension of the subject's alienation from itself that psychoanalysis uncovers. According to Lacan, the Real is at the center of morality: "My thesis is that the moral law, the moral commandment, the presence of the moral instance, is that by which, in our activity in so far as structured by the symbolic, the real presents itself—the real as such, the weight of the real" (VII 28). The thing (*la Chose, das Ding*) orients the subject's desire: "The *Ding* as *Fremde*, strange and even hostile to the occasion, in any case as the first exterior, is that around which the entire progression of the subject orients itself" (VII 63). The thing as "absolutely Other" is that which engages human responsiveness and orients the subject's desire. For Lacan, as interpreter of Freud, the Other is the first outside stimulus that provokes the cry of *You!* or *Me! (Toi! Moi!* VII 69–70), that by which the self overcomes itself in action, the root of morality and ethics.

In Lacan's topography of the *moi* or subject, the thing (*la Chose*) is the exteriority at the core, around which the subject moves, motivated by desire.[7] This topography, at the same time, is Lacan's explication of the moral law. He states: "Already, by nothing more than writing it this way on the blackboard, by placing *das Ding* in the center, and around it the subjective world of the unconscious organized in signifying relations, you will see the difficulty of the representation. Because this *das Ding* is precisely in the center in the sense that it is excluded. *Which is to say that in reality it must be posited as exterior*, this *das Ding*, this prehistoric Other impossible to forget of which Freud affirms for us the necessity of its primary position, in the form of something which is *entfremdet*, strange to me (*moi*) all the while being at the heart of this *moi*, something which at the level of the unconscious, only represents a representation" (VII 87; my italics). At the center of Lacan's graph of the subject is something "exterior" to it, excluded, available to reflection only as "the representation of a representation." This is the same phenomenon of exteriority identified earlier in "La chose freudienne," stemming from specular self-identification. In language close to that of Levinas, Lacan claims Freud insisted that this relation to the absolutely other, the strange, comes *first*. From our previous discussion,

then, what we want to investigate is the position of this primary relation of exteriority to the law. This relation, called desire by both Levinas and Lacan, is central to the views of both on exteriority and
ethics.

Lacan says that the ethical awareness of the subject begins with the
association of the law with its own desire: "[Ethics] begins at the moment when the subject poses the question of this 'good' which it has
sought unconsciously in the social structures—and when, by the same
stroke, it is led to discover the profound link by which that which is
presented to it as law is strictly tied to the structure of desire" (VII 92).
The Symbolic realm in Lacan's thought, always tied to language and
the "nom du père," regulates the social interactions of the subject by
reference to the law. The Imaginary, as the realm of the subject's desire,
is also the level of self-identificatory awareness and mirror stage ego
projection. The Real, or la Chose, with which we began our analysis of
Lacan, is the emptiness or void at the core of the subject around which
the subject's desire moves. If we are to believe the previous statements,
the Real as exteriority comes first. Imaginary self-identification and the
workings of desire are determined through this structure and mediated
by the Symbolic law. We can then establish that for Lacan there can be
no ethics without the strict correlation of law and desire. Both of these
in turn are founded on the profound void at the center of the subject,
"that intimate exteriority, that extimity [sic], which is the Thing" (VII
167; my italics).

It would be hard to imagine a more scathing dissection of Lacan's
theory than Jean-François Lyotard's in his 1971 study, Discours, figure
(esp. DF 250–60), yet the model for nonoppositional difference Lyotard
develops is in many ways continuous with Lacan's theory of exteriority. Much of Lyotard's theoretical grounding is taken from Hegel's
distinction between interiority and exteriority, and its adaptation through
Frege's theory of meaning: "sense as interiority which is signification
(Sinn), and sense as exteriority which is designation (Bedeutung)" (Lyotard, DF 42; see Frege, "Über Sinn und Bedeutung"). The interiority of
sense and exteriority of reference are challenged by Lyotard's discussion of the figural in the work of art and Freud's theory of the role of
discourse in the dream: "Between the opposition of difference, there is
the difference of the textual space and the figural space" (DF 211). What
Lyotard wants to establish is a working model for nonoppositional
difference. He identifies the beginnings of such a nonoppositional dif-

ference in Marx's writings on sexual difference, of which he says: "It matters little what is here discussed, but it matters a great deal what is sought, and that is the possiblity to think a relation without including it in a system of oppositions, i.e., if it is true that thinking and placing an object in such a system are the same thing, the possibility of think-ing a relation without thinking it" (DF 139). I would disagree with Lyotard's statement, and say that it matters a great deal that Marx's reflections are spurred by a reflection on sexual difference, as the dis-cussion later in this chapter of Luce Irigaray's work will demonstrate. It is just this nonoppositional relation of inner to outer that Lyotard locates in Freud's writings on the role of the discursive in dreams and the role of figure in discourse when he argues that "it is my belief that there is figure in discourse and that it is there as a fantasm, while the discourse is in the figure as a dream" (DF 253). The reason Lyotard's analysis breaks with traditional discussions of the relation of word and image is that he reverses the discursive spaces at work in these non-oppositional differences.

The work of art is not a dream, and so the role of image is not simply to satisfy desire, as in the dream (DF 322). Rather, there is a reversal of signifying space, much like the structure of exteriority which is our larger subject here. Lyotard outlines this poetic reversal as follows: "The poetic reversal surely concerns 'form' and 'content': but we now can replace these approximate terms by the pertinent concepts: while the fantasm fills the space of dispossession, the work dispossesses the space of accomplishment. The fantasm makes an opposition with dif-ference; poetics remakes a difference with *that* opposition" (DF 360). This passage requires some explication in order to be useful to our purposes. The distinction between "space of dispossession" and "space of accomplishment" can only be understood along the lines of the model of exteriority developed so far. The space of dispossession is clearly the central void at the center of the subject in Lacan's topology—it is exteriority as such. The work of art uses that exteriority to disori-ent the space of rational understanding. This is the difference between interiority and exteriority that lies at the heart of postmodern poetics.[8]

Lyotard's recent major work, *Le Différend*, takes up the model of difference developed in *Discours, figure*, but with a much clearer ethi-cal dimension.[9] The *différend* of the title refers back to nonopposi-tional difference in the sense of being an unassimilable remainder, similar to what Derrida in *Glas* calls the *reste*. The *différend* is also similar to the *reste* in that it refers to what is at issue in a suit in a court of law, the difference or wrong (tort) at stake in the dispute between two parties. As a definition, we might cite the following: "I would like to call *différend* the case where the plaintiff is robbed of the means of proof and becomes as a result of this fact a victim" (D §12). The irresolvable wrong, the unassimilable remainder, or *reste*, not only leaves the victim in a position that is in a sense outside the law, but also calls into question the larger assumptions, or *métarécits*, upon which such law is based.[10] In the absence of larger structures assuring the legitimacy of judgments and actions, Lyotard calls for a move beyond societal consensus to a "postmodern" conception of justice in the framework of language games.[11]

The smallest unit of meaning in the language game—the model itself obviously derives from Wittgenstein—is the phrase, or statement (D pp. 11–12; trans. p. xiii). For the ethics of this phrase or statement, Lyotard turns to an extended analysis of Levinas (D pp. 163–69; trans. pp. 110–15). In particular, he states: "Such is the universe of the ethical phrase: an I stripped of the illusion of being the sender of phrases, seized by the instant of reception, incomprehensibly. The obligation is immediate, anterior to all intelligence; it resides in the 'welcome of the stranger,' in the call to me, which does more than reverse a preexisting relation, which rather institutes a new universe. This shocking reversal precedes any commentary on the nature of the other, of his/her demand, of my liberty" (D p. 164; trans. p. 111 modified). One would be tempted to question, based on this statement, whether the "ethical statement" also precedes the law, that is, whether Lyotard follows Levinas all the way in the direction of establishing the call of the absolutely other as primary. Certainly the language of this passage recalls the constitution of the subject in Lacan's model. Exteriority is without question the operative structure in the "ethical statement." An important development in Lyotard's thinking on nonoppositional difference and exteriority, which he explores through the *différend*, is the idea of irreversibility, of the fundamental dissymmetry in the ethical instance. This he likewise traces to Levinas: "Levinas tries to break this reversible totality [no interiority without exteriority, and the reverse], to derail speculative logic, by reinforcing the dissymmetry of ethical instances" (D pp. 166–67; trans. p. 113 modified). Lyotard's longstanding association with the philosophy of phenomenology remains evident as we follow the development in his thinking from nonoppositional difference in art and psychoanalysis to the ethical instance at work in the *différend*.[12]

Sexual difference as a nonconceptual, asymmetrical instance of *exteriority* is an insight that Luce Irigaray and other feminist theorists have begun to theorize with great acuity. Levinas early on proposed a view of sexuality as a model for openness to the radically other.[13] And though they do not in any sense take their lead from him, many feminist theorists in recent years have extended this kind of thinking into the very real ethical domains of social equality and justice. Feminist theorists have extended the questioning of gender roles as a social issue to address issues of sexual difference that underlie language and the discursive formations that determine social institutions, or what Derrida would term "writing" in the broader sense. Luce Irigaray is one feminist theorist who takes the work of Levinas very seriously, even as she addresses the question of gender determinations in a writer's discourse.[14] In fact, one of her central theoretical concerns, what she calls the "sexuation of discourse" (CS 71; trans. 73; EDS, 127–28), addresses just the issue of whether a male writer's discourse can ever do an adequate job of representing issues of feminine identity and sexuality. The reverse side perhaps of Irigaray's celebrated notion of *parler femme*, the issue of sexuation of discourse carries a strong theoretical force, particularly in our era.[15]

Philosophy has traditionally worked to efface sexual difference in its discourse as part of its power to *"reduce all others in the economy of the Same"* (CS 72; trans. 74 modified; italics in the original). Importantly for our concerns here, Irigaray even questions if interiority itself is not a male-oriented model of the subject, saying of women generally: "They [women] do not have the interiority that you have, that you perhaps suppose they have" (CS 29; trans. 29). The second half of this sentence reminds one forcefully of Husserl's analogical appresentation which Derrida (oddly) tries to save from Levinas's critique. For Irigaray, the male discourse of psychoanalysis exposes its gender bias primarily with respect to feminine sexual pleasure, or *jouissance*. Her analysis of this tendency leads to her theory of exteriority. She says: "What remains most completely prohibited to woman, of course, is that she should express something of her sexual pleasure. This latter is supposed to remain *a 'realm' of discourse, produced by men*. For in fact feminine pleasure signifies the greatest threat of all to masculine discourse, represents its most irreducible 'exteriority,' or 'exterritoriality'"

(CS 153; trans. 157). This raises the ethical question, for myself at least as a male writer, of whether the entire model of exteriority, as based on nonassimilable difference, is not merely an attempt to appropriate a certain tendency in feminist thought.[16]

Following through on the model of nonoppositional difference derived from Lyotard and others, we can see that sexual difference is just such a difference. Irigaray states, for example, "Rather than maintaining the masculine-feminine opposition, it would be appropriate to see a possibility of *non-hierarchical* articulation of that difference in language" (CS 156–57; trans. 162). In her thinking on sexual difference, Irigaray develops models for interiority and exteriority based on Kant's categories of space and time, identifying time with the interiority of the subject (male) and space with the subject's exteriority (female) (EDS 15). In a move that could be termed either empiricist or essentialist, Irigaray claims support for this distinction in the difference between male and female sex organs and consequent differences in the experience of sexual pleasure. She states: "The man puts infinity in a *transcendent*, always carried over to a beyond, even if the beyond of the concept. The woman puts it in an *expanse* of pleasure here now right away. Body-expanse which tries *to give itself exteriority, to give itself to exteriority*" (EDS 67; italics in the original). As challenging as this line of thinking is, the question remains how Irigaray's distinctions here radically escape the possibility of hierarchy. Her thinking, here as elsewhere, also seems to derive inescapably from a certain empiricism, or essentialism, based on external sexual characteristics. The theoretical power of exteriority, both in her thought and with relation to the other thinkers we have examined, derives from being at the same time both physical and metaphorical, an idea to which Irigaray does assent in places. Notably in her discussion of Descartes on the faculty of admiration (EDS 77), Irigaray comes very close to Levinas's language of being called by the other. This primary relation of exteriority is at the basis of Irigaray's ethics as well.

Avoiding a strictly physical interpretation of sexual difference, while acknowledging its extreme importance for the organization of mental and social structures, means giving the full range to exteriority as an ethical model. Sex differences are a primary confrontation with the absolutely other at the same time as being a type of nonoppositional, nonassimilable difference. What organizes the model is its irreversibility. Taking over the subject-world chiasma of phenomenology, especially in the thinking of Merleau-Ponty, Irigaray's model of exteriority based on sexual difference demonstrates that there can be no absolute exchange—there is always a difference, a *reste*, a remainder. Regarding Merleau-Ponty's philosophy of reversibility, Irigaray states: "Everything is there and nonetheless philosophy has the function of restoring a power of signifying, a birth of sense or a primitive sense. The question is: does this remain possible without changing the foundations of language? Without lifting the hypothesis that *reversibility* is the ultimate truth? A hypothesis which must be interrogated and 'opened' in order for there to be born a sense until now unheard(-of), that of a sexuated language and encountering in the word and in the world a sex which is *irreducible* to it and with which it is impossible to have relations of reversibility without remainder (*reste*)" (EDS 171). The breakthrough in Merleau-Ponty's phenomenology constituted by his attention to the body-subject is here given still fuller scope. Irreversibility is Irigaray's means of expressing the exteriority that is both constitutive of the subject and a primary aspect of our existence as sexed beings: as such it also constitutes a continuing ethical challenge.

The thought of Levinas on exteriority, and those thinkers who directly or indirectly follow and extend his thinking, uncovers the necessary ethical dimension to the theory of difference. The ethics of sexual difference that is Irigaray's primary focus serves both as paradigm and unassimilable remainder. Ultimately, such difference cannot be completely conceptualized. Rather the view of the subject such a project urges is one that sees the subject inextricably a part of a relational structure in which the notions of complete transparency or reversibility do not hold. Called by the other *first*, the subject must remain open to this ethical demand, recognizing in the other not merely an alter ego but an other who is truly other, on whom the subject's freedom depends.

Chapter Five

The Ethical Feminism of Julia Kristeva

Feminism is essentially an ethical discourse, a movement within society to change the ways one should act. This primary injunction of feminist discourse is a source of power and change—the basis of feminist politics. In fact, one might follow Alice Jardine's challenging notion in *Gynesis* that all modernist thinking—though usually not conscious of doing so—is thinking the question of woman, and argue that feminist theory represents within modernist thinking a return to ethics, a return with a difference. In saying this, one would be reiterating a position outlined by Julia Kristeva when she declares at the end of her "Stabat Mater" that "if an ethics of modernity is no longer to be confused with morality its reformulation demands a place for women [si une éthique de la modernité ne se confond plus avec la moralité alors sa reformulation exige la part des femmes]" (HA 247; TL 262 [trans. modified]). Yet despite Kristeva's prominence in the theoretical discourse, there exists no clear agreement that her work is even feminist, much less that her writings should be acknowledged as pointing the way for current feminist thinking.[1] In arguing for Kristeva's inescapable place in any account of "ethical feminism," I am therefore arguing for her distinctive place within the discourses of feminism as well as her usefulness for negotiating an ethics of critical practice.[2]

Kristeva has maintained, of course, a certain distance from what we might want to call the feminist movement (*le mouvement de libération des femmes,* MLF). At times her resistance has even sounded rather strident: "Leaving aside adherents of a feminism that is jealous of conserving its power—the last of the power-seeking ideologies—none will accuse of being a usurper the artist who, even if he or she does not know it, is an undoer of narcissism and of all imaginary identity as well, sexual included [Il n'y aura qu'un féminisme jaloux de préserver son pouvoir—dernière des idéologies revendicatrices de pouvoir—pour crier à l'usurpateur devant cet artiste qui, même s'il ignore, est un défaiseur de narcissisme comme de toute identité imaginaire, y compris sexuelle]" (PH 246; trans. 208 modified). Here, at the end of her book on abjection, *Pouvoirs de l'horreur* (*Powers of Horror*), Kristeva feels compelled to address her accusers. She seeks to separate her discourse in a distinctive manner from certain other discourses claiming feminist goals. I have elsewhere termed the discourse, which Kristeva here disdains, *normative* feminism. I will try to outline briefly the distinction between *normative* and *ethical* feminism, before returning to develop the role of artistic expression in what Jardine, following Kristeva, has termed "the negativization of narcissism within a practice" (Jardine, OT 109; Kristeva, RLP 203, trans. 233).

Feminism can be seen as normative in several different ways. As I stated at the outset, feminism is a normative discourse because it is above all ethical, a movement within society to change prevailing gender norms and behaviors. At the level of the university, feminist activity is not only a theoretical concern, but a historical and sociological phenomenon: addressing forthrightly the need for leadership roles of women within the academy, insisting on the place for female-authored texts in the canon, urging that we recognize the different needs of women students and teachers. The partial successes of the feminist movement in all of these areas need to be celebrated, at the same time as we reaffirm the political activity that remains necessary to achieve these goals more fully. Yet even critics who are not themselves "normative" feminists are compelled to recognize how feminism is normative today within the academy as it has come to be "one of the few viable critical discourses around" (Jardine, *Gynesis* 63).

Those critics whom I view as "normative" feminists are so because they maintain a "normative" position on language itself.[3] I focus the discussion here on Gilbert and Gubar's recent work, in part because of their cultural prominence and in part because their political position is so clearly stated. The language of literary expression used by women both can and ought to represent their specific, gendered experience, according to Gilbert and Gubar. In so doing, women literary artists are fighting a battle against the tradition of the male modernists whose literary practices amount to a "reaction-formation against the rise of literary women" (156). Arguing against Kristeva's theory, common to the whole range of Lacanian thinking, that the subject is alienated from itself in the accession to language during the Oedipal stage, Gilbert and Gubar propose a model in which language is both nonalienated and essential to gendered experience. They claim that "women need not experience any ontological alienation from the idea of language as we know it" (265). Kristeva is thus a double enemy of women. For one, she upholds the Freudian/Lacanian position on gender differences and the resulting alienation of the subject in language. What's more, she celebrates the work of male modernist writers who engage in experimental language practices that are, in their very essence, masculinist attacks on language itself as the "mother tongue" (Gilbert and Gubar 251–62). To give voice to the counterargument to this position, we might repeat with Kristeva that these critics are indeed "jealous" of any attempts to usurp their power—in fact, their discourse, which Kristeva has described in advance, is based on just such a theory of narcissistic wounding and counterattack. The real question is whether the model of "normative" language underlying this account of literary history gets us anywhere. The critical *différend* between Kristeva and the "normative" feminists is whether critical theory is itself a matter of choice, as Gilbert and Gubar claim. Whereas Gilbert and Gubar would claim that if we don't like such ideas as castration anxiety, separation from the mother, and the domination of the signifier in the unconscious, we can just choose to believe in our own fantasy-creation, Kristeva believes that these aspects of the psychoanalytic theory are inescapable.[4]

The place to begin exploring this difference is narcissism. Gilbert and Gubar subscribe to Harold Bloom's position that narcissism is the motor of artistic production because it locates a self that can make critical/poetic choices. As Bloom says: "The mystery of poetic style, the exuberance that is beauty in every strong poet, is akin to the mature ego's delight in its own individuality, which reduces to the mystery of narcissism" (146). Kristeva's work of the past twenty years has been directed at a deep reading of the psychic forces that would reverse this notion of narcissism as "the mature ego's delight in its own individuality" (whatever that might be). As she says in *Histoires d'amour*: "The death drive and its psychological equivalent, hatred, is what Freud discovers after stopping off at Narcissus. Narcissism and its lining, emptiness, are in short our most intimate, brittle, and archaic elaborations of the death drive. The most advanced, courageous, and threat-

ened sentries of primal repression [La pulsion de mort, et son équiva-
lent psychologique, la haine, est ce que Freud découvrira après s'être
arrêté chez Narcisse. Le narcissisme et sa doublure, le vide, sont en
somme nos élaborations les plus intimes, les plus fragiles et les plus
archaïques, de la pulsion de mort. Les vigiles les plus avancés, les plus
courageux et les plus menacés, du refoulement originaire]" (HA 47; TL
43–44). Kristeva had by this point already explored the maternal component of primary narcissism in her vital and still widely misunderstood
work on abjection. Here, however, the stakes are clear: Is narcissism
something to be celebrated, exalted, placed at the center of artistic
production, and, for feminists following this model, at the center of
feminist theory? Or is it our primal link with our own death urge, so
deeply repressed that to confront it (outside the realm of art or analysis,
and sometimes even there) plunges the subject into abject suffering
and depression?

What is at stake in the reception of Kristeva's work is the complex
interrelation of the aesthetic and ideological implications of her psychoanalytic theory. I take issue, for example, with Alice Jardine's quick
and emphatic statement that Kristeva's work on abjection in *Pouvoirs
de l'horreur* is centered exclusively on the male psyche: "In her book,
Pouvoirs de l'horreur, Kristeva explored what she sees as the fundamental condition of late-twentieth-century man—and by man, she means
men: Abjection" (OT 112). At this stage, according to Kristeva, the very
young child is trying to define the limits of his or her body as a prelimi-
nary stage in developing a self-contained identity. The extremely young
child, or *infans* (literally, without speech), accomplishes this in part by
ab-jecting, or dismissing with an attitude of disgust, those liminal
preobjects such as saliva, vomit, excrement, or curdled mother's milk
that have a borderline status between what is part of one's own/clean
body, or *corps propre*, and what is not.[5] As Kristeva's subsequent work
in *Histoires d'amour* (*Tales of Love*) and *Soleil noir* (*Black Sun*) has
shown, the uncovering of the mechanism of abjection was a necessary
step leading into her work on love and depression, and specifically
women's depression (see especially, *Soleil noir*, section 3).[6] Jardine's
statement implies that the analysis of Céline in *Pouvoirs de l'horreur* is
paradigmatic only of male writers. But since Kristeva's strategy has
increasingly been to address psychoanalytical issues through artistic
means, it is important not to reinscribe the male-author model that
feminist criticism has worked so hard to challenge.[7]

Abjection is a primary stage tied to narcissism and thus the mirror stage of Lacan's formulation. We have already reviewed Kristeva's statement on the foundations of narcissism in primal repression. Not only is the role of the mother in the stage of abjection a key to understanding what Kristeva is after here, it is crucial to see that, in Kristeva's view, women are throughout their lives structurally *closer* to abjection than are men. Within Kristeva's metapsychic model, this explains the structural position of the female subject *before* the gender differences traditionally traced to the Oedipal stage. This stance reveals her fundamental difference from the theories of both Freud and Lacan. Men clearly also have a problem when the stage of abjection becomes primary in later life—hence the significance of Kristeva's treatment of Céline's work.[8] With women the stage of abjection is an ongoing struggle that is most often manifested in much less perceptible but no less corrosive ways, particularly in "borderline" states. The recent evidence pointing to the disproportionate number of women who suffer from clinical depression would be one index of this, although battery and poverty certainly must be taken into account as well. The unresolved relationship Kristeva posits for Céline and his mother revolves at least in part around the feminization Céline thought he had experienced. Kristeva provides an explanation for why daughters experience more difficulty achieving separation from their mothers that Freud could not (WT 204), especially given the "sexuation" of his discourse that Irigaray outlines.[9]

If our earliest attempts at self-differentiation are those by which we attempt to ab-ject those borderline preobjectal objects, and if the identificatory core of these experiments in abjection is the maternal body (see Oliver 55–61), then Kristeva's model of abjection certainly goes far beyond selected male-authored literary texts. This mechanism is meant to account for religious proscriptions of food and other kinds of "uncleanliness"—many having to do with women, of course—that still order our cultural categories (see PH, ch. 3), as well as psychological manifestations of "borderline" behavior. But I follow Shuli Barzilai, among others, who sees in Kristeva's move to the prelinguistic, maternal stage not only an attempt to revise the linguistic bias of Lacan but also to refound the bases of psychoanalytic practice in a way that yields unprecedented access to structures of mother-child identification, both mother-son *and* mother-daughter.[10] For Kristeva, this move to the maternal, presymbolic stage is not a choice. She sees the need to theorize abjection as historically contingent, a necessary response to the suffering of those in our culture—many of them women, as the increasing space Kristeva devotes to her patients' narratives demonstrates—who are psychically unable to love, emotionally unable to form real attachments (obviously speaking about both men and women). As those who work in the clinical field know all too well, the condition of the "borderline" patient is both statistically and in "real" terms the predominant form of illness in today's society.

Kristeva's advance is to give us not only a "viable" discourse concerning the early stages of psychic development, a discourse that is moreover an exemplary kind of feminist practice, but also to link her analytic insights to artistic practice. For Kristeva increasingly means to demonstrate through her writings that art in our culture can exercise an "analytic" function, where "analytic" in this formulation means something like therapeutic. Kristeva's discourse points to an ethical direction for feminism, as opposed to the "normative" feminism she sees as striving for a position of cultural dominance. Her ethical feminism also points to an important possible avenue for thinking the ethical subject of discourse in the context of the current return to ethical criticism.

Kristeva announced relatively early on her stance that ethics is tied to a textual practice, especially at the end of the main theoretical section of *Révolution du langage poétique,* where she states: "'Ethics' should be understood here to mean the negativizing of narcissism within a *practice;* in other words, a practice is ethical when it dissolves those narcissistic fixations . . . to which the signifying process succumbs in its socio-symbolic realization [Nous entendrons par *éthique* la négativation du narcissisme dans une *pratique;* autrement dit, est éthique une pratique qui dissout les fixations narcissiques . . . auxquelles succombe le procès signifiant dans son effectuation socio-symbolique]" (RLP 203; trans. 233; cf. Jardine, OT 109). Narcissism here is aligned with the *symbolic* as opposed to the *semiotic* in Kristeva's celebrated distinction between these two signifying functions. Narcissism, as discussed earlier as that which allows the subject to effectuate primal repression, seems in this passage to be tied to those "fixations" of the ego-identity that move in the realm of the symbolic law. Kristeva consistently rejects any ethics founded on a universal law, whether Kantian or Hegelian: "Finally, our notion of the ethical as coextensive with textual practice separates us from the 'scientific morality' that would like to found a normative, albeit apparently libertarian, ethics based on knowledge [Enfin, notre conception de l'éthique comme co-extensive à la pratique textuelle, nous sépare de la 'morale scientifique' qui veut fonder une éthique normative, bien qu'apparemment libertaire, à base de connaissance]" (RLP 204; trans. 234). Here normative has the larger sense it has in common usage, rather than the limited sense of "normative" language practice I have ascribed to some kinds of feminist theory; but still it is clear that Kristeva rejects any kind of normative ethics. Just what a nonnormative ethics might be is pointed to in the *Révolution* as a certain kind of textual practice, giving free rein to the semiotic in the elaboration of poetic forms.[11] Nonnormative ethics in her subsequent work has taken the form of opposing the analytic/ artistic practice to socially normative discourses of power, politics, and the symbolic generally.[12]

Just where does Kristeva's ethical thinking fit in the overall range of work representing what I am here calling the "return" to ethical criticism, especially among Anglophone critics? One place to begin might be the surge of interest in the ethical aspect of deconstruction, including the ethical theories of Paul de Man. In *Allegories of Reading*, de Man claims: "Allegories are always ethical, the term ethical designating the structural interference of two distinct value systems" (206). One sees here the typical de Manian rhetorical stance, wanting to pose conflicting systems of meaning which can then be used to mutually undercut each other. The extension of these kinds of gestures being practiced under the name of deconstruction becomes that much clearer if we examine Hillis Miller's work that seems to promise an ethics of deconstruction, *The Ethics of Reading*. As opposed to the critics whom I will be discussing shortly, Miller claims that narratives are ethical not because we see in them the depiction of situations with which we might identify, but because of the nature of language itself: "It is not because stories contain the thematic dramatization of ethical situations, choices, and judgments that they are especially appropriate for my topic, but . . . because ethics itself has a peculiar relation to that form of language we call narrative. The thematic dramatizations of ethical topics in narratives are the oblique allegorizations of this linguistic necessity" (3). This "linguistic necessity" is, as Werner Hamacher says, following de Man, "a character of language itself, that is, a necessary trait that first makes language language at all" (Hamacher 185). Now this sounds as if it might get us somewhere, perhaps even into the domain of the languages of art in their analytic function that Kristeva has proposed. But in fact Miller resolves his argument with a rather weakly restated Kantianism, so that he can perform his typically de Manian category reversal: "Well, if ethics has nothing to do with any of the things it has traditionally been thought to be concerned with, with what then does it have to do? The answer is that ethical judgment and command is a necessary feature of human language. We cannot help making judgments of right and wrong, commanding others to act according to those judgments, condemning them for not doing so, responding ourselves to an ethical demand that will not be the less categorical and imperative for not coming from some transcendent extra-linguistic 'law'" (46). Ethics, in Miller's version of deconstruction, is resituated in language itself, rather than in a Kantian moral imperative; but its effects remain virtually, even banally, the same. From my perspective, if there is such a thing as ethical deconstruction, Miller's approach is not it.[13]

The version of deconstruction that we might, generally speaking, call de Manian, with its ultimately static view of the ethics of language as yet another form of endless regress, seems to be what other critics, in their push to restore "ethical" criticism, want to counter. Wayne Booth, in *The Company We Keep*, begins by tracing the decline of ethical criticism in the past thirty or forty years. Oddly, he seems to have no conception of the role of Nietzsche's thinking in rendering any ethical system based on a hierarchy of values suspect for several generations of European thinkers, among whom we must include Kristeva. In fact, Booth's whole procedure in his review of the recent criticism, including what seem to me deliberate misreadings of figures like Derrida and Bakhtin, could be characterized as what he calls, admittedly in a different context, "'unethical' ethical criticism" (151). When it comes time to outline what an ethical criticism would look like, he develops the by-now well-known idea of authors as "friends."[14] I note here only that this concept depends on the kind of normative ethics that Kristeva has placed in radical question, that is, a comparative "logic we depend on as we arrive at our particular appraisals" (Booth 71). Based then entirely on cognitive, rule-bound behaviors, there should be no surprise when Booth's methodology fails to produce a model that can account for the presence of powerful emotional, psychic, and intersubjective forces in literary works. It seems to be too late for a return to an Aristotelian model of ethical literary practice, even if that model had been totally convincing in the first place.

Charles Altieri's recent work on ethical criticism, *Canons and Conse-quences,* does not make the same mistake of overlooking deconstruc-tion. He wants to claim a basis in Wittgenstein for his understanding of the language games that constitute literary works: "Wittgenstein's un-derstanding of understanding will eventually allow us to give cogent support to traditional claims that literary works serve distinct cogni-tive and normative roles" (83). Altieri acknowledges that Derrida, Foucault, and others (among whom we must include Kristeva) have rejected the claims of a universal reason, and therefore a universalist ethics: "Thus, while [Derrida] shares Foucault's distrust of basing an ethics on any general political or social claims, he develops an equation between responsiveness and responsibility that is committed to ver-sions of nonviolence entailing resistance to a wide range of social ar-rangements" (213). Altieri here seems to be aware at least of the possi-bilities offered by what I have been calling so far a nonnormative ethics, or, alternatively, ethical deconstruction. In a rather wistful footnote, Altieri even bows in the direction of Kristeva's recent work, without however taking it up (339n). But, as in his other work, Altieri wants to cling to his idea of personhood as a locus of values. The person or self thus becomes a repository for values established through communal means, including art: "The major influence of aesthetic theory here is on how we choose to specify what holds a community together so that we internalize its role as a normative ground in our acts of judgment" (249). A statement like this one shows the appeal of Altieri's formula-tions, were it only possible to hold to his notion of judgment based on "normative grounds," which at least from the Kristevan perspective is no longer a cultural possiblity.[15]

I could go on in this review of the various positions taken by critics who want to claim the ethical as their primary domain.[16] At some point, though, we must ask: Does the model of judgment that is upheld by critics as different from each other as Booth and Altieri work when dealing with what each would recognize as the expressive force of works of art? The de Manian school of deconstruction would say of course not, that judgment is always undercut by the conflicting systems that constitute language and make language itself "ethical." Those of us who want to save deconstruction from the deconstructors see a need to resist this mystification; but do we thus need a return to stable Aris-totelian values, as in Booth, or to a stable "person" as locus of values, as in Altieri, or to a stable, representative language, as in Gilbert and

Gubar? The question needs to be reposed, to ask: What is it in the literary work or other forms of art that our "ethical" criticism should allow us to uncover or propose as a value? Here, Kristeva's theory offers a powerful alternative both to the undecidability theory of the de Manians *and* to the normative values underlying much other English-language criticism. Kristeva's analyses allow us to see an "analytic" function in works by such diverse writers as Dostoevsky, Céline, and Marguerite Duras, for example, that nothing in the normative tradition, not even Altieri's formulations, can come close to reaching. Altieri repeatedly cites Longinus's passage in which the classical philosopher says we should learn how to act by comparing our acts to the great actions of those who cross the stage of the past, but nowhere does Altieri acknowledge the strange, fundamentally altering, noncognitive effects of the *sublime* which, after all, is Longinus's principal concern. Kristeva, through her depth psychoanalytical approach, gives us something like a postmodern view of the *sublime*—seen from the reverse angle of abjection, depression, and madness.

In order to demonstrate the potential value of Kristeva's depth psychoanalytical position, I want to offer one kind of feminist reading of the recent film, *The Silence of the Lambs* (1991), in part because others have already identified its potential status as a feminist work. What I am offering here as a view of Kristeva's theory of analytic/artistic practice should not be seen, however, as just another return to the aesthetics of the irrational. Rita Kempley's opening-day review of *The Silence of the Lambs* contained the suggestive comment that this slickly produced horror movie might even be considered feminist. Clarice Starling, the film's protagonist, is an FBI agent-in-training who is summoned to participate in the search for clues in the case of a serial killer, nicknamed "Buffalo Bill." Her special in is to be her possible rapport with another serial killer, the incarcerated Dr. Hannibal Lecter, or "Hannibal the Cannibal." Through her conversations with Dr. Lecter, Starling does indeed develop clues that lead her to the identity and eventual apprehension of "Buffalo Bill." Starling's role in his capture is highlighted by her independence, her intelligence, and her femaleness. This accounts, I think, for Kempley's claim that the film could be seen as a feminist work.

As appealing as this reading might be, I think that *The Silence of the Lambs* is essentially a subversive film, one in which American culture in late capitalism is seen as pervasively threatening and violent, especially toward women. The character of Clarice Starling is not so much an empowered woman, although the elements for such a characterization are clearly there and necessary for a successful identification by both female and male viewers.[17] She is rather a virgin to horror who in the course of the film loses this virginity. Céline, in his *Voyage au bout de la nuit*, says, in a phrase that is picked up by Kristeva: "One is a virgin to horror, as one is a virgin to love [On est puceau de l'horreur comme on est puceau de la volupté]" (Kristeva, PH 164; trans. modified 140). Céline, of course, is talking about his experience as a soldier in World War I; and, as such, *puceau* does not refer specifically to women. (The feminine form, *pucelle*, occurs much more frequently, both in common and in literary usage.) Kristeva, as we have seen, concentrates on the mechanism of *abjection* in Céline's work as a way of accounting for the fear and loathing that Céline experiences and/or writes out of. But I have also argued that women are not excluded from the mechanism of abjection, as claimed by Jardine, but are structurally *closer* to abjection in Kristeva's theoretical model.

Despite the early consensus in reviews that Dr. Lecter's profession as a psychiatrist is a plot-driven coincidence, I think it is no accident. Not only do his professional capabilities allow him to get under Starling's skin, so to speak, during their interviews, but the psychoanalytic discourse itself as it emerges in the film is focused at the very early childhood level, the pre-Oedipal stage of attachment to the mother where Kristeva locates abjection. A key to Starling's personal psychology is that she is essentially motherless ("My mother died when I was very young"), and then orphaned through the violent shooting death of her father, a town marshall. Upon losing both parents, the ten-year-old girl is sent to live with her mother's cousin and her husband on a ranch in Montana. In a central memory from childhood, Starling remembers waking in the night to hear crying, the crying of the spring lambs being slaughtered. She rises and attempts to free the lambs, but failing at this, she takes one lamb in her arms and starts to run away. She is apprehended a short distance down the road and the rancher is so angry that the young girl is sent to live in an orphanage in Bozeman. Lecter, shrewd psychiatrist that he is, recognizes that Starling's driving desire to free the young woman being held captive by "Buffalo Bill" is a cathected form of her desire to stop the lambs from crying.

The horror generated in the film needs this Imaginary component in order to transcend the exploitation of the horror-film genre (see Clover

232–33). Viewers of the film several times see Lecter's mouth restrained with baroque devices that somewhat resemble the muzzles used for dogs. These muzzles are supposed to prevent him from chewing on people as he is interviewed or transported from place to place; what they also do is focus on the level of his utterance. Many people in responding to the film remark on the haunting quality of Anthony Hopkins' voice. During Lecter's interviews with Starling, he forces her to accept a mode of *quid pro quo*, asking her questions about herself such as (referring to the rancher): "Did he sodomize you?" The United States senator whose daughter is being held by "Bill" is, interestingly, a woman and it is she who provides Lecter with a special dispensation so that he will cooperate with the investigation. When she finally sees him, however, she is revolted. Lecter provokes her ire in particular by questioning whether she breast-fed her daughter and, if so, whether her nipple now hurts, reminding her of her daughter's plight. The senator indicates the limitations of the "normative" sociosymbolic position. She may be the model of the "concerned mother," but neither that concern, nor her position of political power, will suffice. At the very least, her character demonstrates the film's ambiguous depiction of the kind of role-model feminism which, I take it, Kempley sees the film as advocating. Lecter's questions to the senator and to Starling are properly formed utterances and so might in other circumstances qualify as part of the psychoanalytic discourse. Yet, because of his muzzle and his straitjacket, Lecter is "outside" the sociosymbolic discourse and his utterances become transgressive. The cannibal-psychiatrist's questions to the senator and the young FBI agent return insistently to the stage of the mother-child attachment, the stage at which Kristeva locates abjection. Human flesh, once one is fully socialized in our culture, is well beyond the accepted limits of what counts as proper nourishment. Lecter's cannibalism, hinted at more than shown, transgresses those limits in ways that parallel his transgression of the limits of the analytical encounter.

Because abjection and horror are prediscursive stages of development, they are hard to get at through discursive means. This is one reason, I would hypothesize, why the pervasive terror many women in our culture sometimes feel, combined feelings of danger and powerlessness, can be hard to articulate. One way to articulate these feelings is in disgust with male sexuality generally. *The Silence of the Lambs* certainly contains elements that would coincide with such an *en masse* rejection of male sexuality. "Buffalo Bill" is a faux transsexual who abducts and murders women so that he can make himself a suit out of pieces of their skin. Starling is "hit on" by a variety of male characters, perhaps the most endearing (that is, the least dangerous) being the nerdy entomologists she enlists to identify a death's head moth found lodged in one victim's throat. And yet Starling, significantly, remains virginal in sexual terms. This is an underlying, or unconscious if you will, reason for Kempley's characterization of the film as feminist. But such a rejection would not constitute a therapeutic move in Kristeva's sense of the alliance between analysis and art (cf. WT, 207).[18]

There is a therapeutic angle to the depiction of abjection in *The Silence of the Lambs*. "Buffalo Bill" is a case study in abjection, not a true transsexual, according to Lecter (who saw him as a patient), but someone who has been made into a murderer through years of abuse. That the abuse was directed at him from his seamstress mother is hinted at by elements of the plot, including his twisted obsession with sewing. Kristeva quotes Céline as saying that he was "one of the rare men" who could tell the infinitesimal differences between different kinds of lace—because his mother trained him well, oh so well (PH 185; trans. 157). The young kidnapping and potential murder victim that "Bill" keeps in an *oubliette* is a visual image of abjection. In fact, one could probably say that the young female victim is the male sadist's abjected vision of himself on some level of his psyche, this image in turn stemming from his own childhood abuse. Or, as Kristeva says, in relation to Céline's narrative practice: "His whole narrative stance seems controlled by the necessity of going through abjection, whose intimate side is suffering and horror its public feature [toute la position narrative semble commandée par la nécessité de traverser l'abjection dont la douleur est le côté intime, et l'horreur le visage public]" (PH 165; trans. 140). Dr. Lecter, the cannibal psychiatrist, is in some ways *beyond* this dichotomy of good and evil, inside and outside. ("They don't have a name for what he is," Starling tells a spooked officer.) Starling's extended encounters with Dr. Lecter lead to a kind of analytical *transference* (admittedly of the nonstandard variety), a transference that allows her to accompany him through the wall constituting the boundaries of "normal" morality. But she comes back from the other side with an increased effectiveness in her work and an increased sense of her own deeper identity. This is why *The Silence of the Lambs* is a feminist text: Starling faces up to the abjection of "Bill" and his female victim by facing her own deepest psychic formations, and reemerging with the "cure."[19]

Such are the powers of horror. Any ethical criticism and especially any feminist criticism that claims ethical ends must account for the less-than-noble characteristics of both men and women. But here I've fallen into the proscriptive trap of setting out normative goals and behaviors.[20] Kristeva's keenest insight may be that we must resist this urge as much as possible though, of course, her whole *oeuvre* constitutes a certain set of validated behaviors, as does anyone's. Kristeva's nonnormative ethics of practice, both analytic and artistic, emerges as an exemplary attempt to think ethics ethically. Perhaps it should be clear by now that the "ethical feminism" of my chapter title is something of a pleonasm. For it is my view that feminism is quite simply one name for ethical practice in our time.

Chapter Six

Deconstruction's "Impossible" Ethics

Two questions will help to determine the parameters of the discussion to follow in the next two chapters. One of these questions is: *What is intersubjective violence?* And the other question is: *Is Derrida pointing to a kind of ethics that in practice would be unattainable?* As the discussion in the chapter on difference indicated, Derrida in the *Grammatology* suggests "intersubjective violence" as the horizon for thinking "writing" in the expanded sense he has catachrestically given it. This operation of the trace as *différance* is one way of talking about the workings of the written sign, but the trace is also what ensures that this effacement of prior meanings is a violent process. The expansion of the term "writing" to stand for the workings of all institutions of human culture—including, but not limited to, economic, religious, and political systems—whether these are based on scriptural notation or not, helps to highlight this endless process of differing and deferral of meaning that "is" writing. I see intersubjective violence in this sense as an operation that we can say some concrete things about, although it is so ubiquitous—indeed, it involves the working of every function that Derrida identifies as writing—that it is necessarily difficult to define. This inevitable difficulty in defining intersubjective violence is a direct corollary to the rejection of any discourse concerning ethics that could become normative in the sense developed in the previous chapter, any discourse that would serve to tell us what to do under a universalizing set of rules.[1] The ethics of deconstruction are "impossible" for exactly this reason. I would propose here that *ethical deconstruction consists in a self-articulating resistance to intersubjective violence,* which can never become a set of normative or prescriptive rules because any such rules participate in the systems of writing always (already) caught in the systemic violence they would oppose.[2]

Deconstruction's Other: Critical Discourse on Derrida

As Derrida's own work in recent years has tended to invoke the ethical dimension of theory and the sociopolitical realm to which it always must in some sense be responding, considerable attention has been paid to what he has called "an ethic of discussion" (*Limited Inc.* 111–60). My discussion here of the "impossible" ethics of deconstruction begins by examining the violence done to Derrida's thinking by those who would represent themselves as his leading interpreters. Along the way, it will be possible to show how the violence done to Derrida's discourse is inevitably linked to real intersubjective violence, that is, states of affairs in which actually existing individuals are done harm. This is one way to respond to critics such as Christopher Norris, who want to claim real-world effects for deconstruction. As the analysis of his work in my introduction showed, Norris has introduced laudable goals in the discourse surrounding deconstruction, despite the unworkable alliance he proposes between Derrida's work and the social-communication theories of Jürgen Habermas, and despite Norris's attempt to minimize the importance of the work of Heidegger to Derrida's ongoing thinking. Here, I concentrate on the austerely analytical interpretation of Derrida's work offered by Rodolphe Gasché, in contrast to the radical nominalist position of Richard Rorty. Neither of these two alternatives, which between them would present themselves as covering the entire interpretive spectrum, adequately account for the real-world implications of Derrida's thinking that Norris's writings, for example, have called for. The further, serious irony that emerges is that these leading interpreters of Derrida's discourse, by invoking certain kinds of language and thought gestures, actually reinforce and reinscribe real-world conditions of intersubjective violence.

Rodolphe Gasché is one of Derrida's leading interpreters, and his book *The Tain of the Mirror* is one of the most sustained attempts to place Derrida's writings in the context of a "serious" philosophical tradition.[3] Indeed, Gasché proposes to develop "*more rigorous criteria* for any future discussion of Derrida's thought" (9; my italics). In practice, it means reading Derrida's work within a tradition of Hegelian scholarship, in which Hegel's development of the "philosophy of reflection" is viewed as not only the most successful version of that philosophical tradition, but also as providing an ongoing model for any philosophical project claiming any kind of serious treatment of the thinking and judging subject. Ironically, Derrida's most sustained treatment of Hegel's philosophy, *Glas* (1974), is excluded from Gasché's discussion.[4] Gasché notes this exclusion as follows: "As a matter of fact, this book is based on almost the entirety of Derrida's writing up to *La vérité en peinture* (1979)—with the exception of *Glas*—as well as on a host of essays" (4). Although Gasché does not say so directly, this exclusion is based on his distinction between those works by Derrida he views as "philosophically discursive" and those he views as more "literary" or "playful" (4; Gasché places quotation marks around the two latter terms, but not the former). This stance meshes with Gasché's later, dismissive contention that "Derrida's marked interest in literature, an interest that began with his questioning the particular ideality of literature, has in his thinking never led to anything remotely resembling literary criticism or to a valorization of what literary critics agree to call literature" (255).[5] If Gasché were not so opposed to the literary, one would even have to call this hyperbole. Thus, the "playful" text of *Glas* (Gasché's implied designation) is doubly disqualified, since in addition to being Derrida's most sustained treatment of Hegel's philosophy, specifically his social and moral philosophy, it is also, in its treatment of the works of Jean Genet, one of Derrida's most sustained treatments of a single literary figure.[6] The question that emerges is whether this double exclusion leaves any marks or traces in Gasché's text.

As it happens, otherness, difference, and exclusion, the whole complex of which Gasché terms "heterology," is one of Gasché key organizing themes. The discussion of "heterology" in turn leads to what Gasché terms Derrida's "infrastructures," transcendental preconditions of discursive functioning. Gasché locates Derrida's thinking on difference in relation to Heidegger's, which in turn must be related to the philosophy of self-reflection that is Gasché's overall subject. So we find Gasché saying, for example, "What distinguishes Heidegger's and Derrida's positions from that of idealist philosophy is primarily their inquiry into what may be called the difference between identity and difference, between the totality of what is and the difference that inhabits self-relation" (87). This previously unthought difference is what we might call, following Gasché, "radical" alterity, and a key question for Gasché thus becomes how to account for this radical alterity within the philosophy of reflection. His conclusion to this chapter on heterology is elegant, and seems to find a nice resolution to this problem in his philosophical inquiry. Gasché states: "This alterity forever undermines, but also makes possible, the dream of autonomy achieved through a reflexive coiling upon self, since it names a structural precondition of such a desired state, a precondition that represents the limit of such a possiblity" (105). In this way, Derrida's *différance* functions in Gasché's model as an infrastructure, a precondition to certain kinds of philosophical thinking. The resulting description of Derrida's project, however, is highly abstract—to the point of leaving behind any possibility for dealing with anything like real-world conditions.

At the center of Gasché's discussion of Derrida's heterology there is a complex discussion of the relation of Derrida's thinking to Plato's theory of weaving together of different strands, or *symploke*. Gasché relates this to Derrida's thinking on difference as "radical" alterity, as this extended excerpt from Gasché's discussion shows:

> *Symploke* can achieve its goal only if it expels from the envisoned totality those opposites that cannot be determined in terms of negativity, that is, in terms of dialectical Otherness. The true statesman, in order to achieve the finest and best of all fabrics in which opposed strands are unified in one organic whole, is bound to eliminate those irreducible Others that do not bend to negativity. Thus, for instance, those children who 'cannot be taught to be courageous and moderate and to acquire the other virtuous tendencies, but are impelled to godlessness and to vaunting pride and injustice by the drive of an evil nature. These the king expels from the community. He puts them to death or banishes them or else he chastises them by the severest public disgrace' ([Plato's *Statesman*, Hamilton and Cairns edition] 308e). The totality woven by the *symploke*—a totality of concurring and complementary opposites—is thus a function of the expulsion of absolute heterogeneity. (97)

This passage represents a dense and, in its way, brilliant discussion of a crucial concept in Plato, building, in its ratiocinative structures, upon the previous discussion of Hegel's concept of negativity and leading to the discussion of Derrida's and Heidegger's notion of radical alterity, as we have seen. But Gasché's totally abstract discourse completely misses, in fact, ignores, erases, banishes, the content of the quoted passage from Plato. Gasché discusses the ideal statesman's actions concerning the "bad boys" of Plato's Greece *neither* for a concrete, literal meaning, *nor* as a metaphor or analogy. The actual example in Plato's text does not rise to the level of notice in Gasché's argument structure. Blind to the playful or literary side of Derrida's discourse, Gasché—at least here—is equally blind to the literal content of the philosopher's discourse. Why even introduce a passage such as this one from Plato and not discuss what it contains, aside from the guiding conceptual thread that in turn serves to link it to the development of a high-level philosophical inquiry?

All the young Jean Genets of Plato's Greece, so indescribably bad and incorrigible, what happens to them? Plato certainly gives a few creative alternatives. And Genet, in his own way, deals with all of these alternatives in the most profound, even religious, manner. Having been subjected to each of the solutions, with the notable exception of death, he was certainly in a fine position to do so, and his literary talents were likewise more than up to the task. If Derrida's *Glas* is meant to demonstrate anything, it is that the case of Genet (*le cas Genet*) stands forever outside the totalizing system of Hegel's philosophy and so *wrecks* its totalizing claims.[7] This would then stand as the "real" reason why Gasché declines to discuss *Glas*—he can't salvage his idea of Derrida as working out the transcendental (or philosophy of reflection) tradition of Hegel if he takes this text into account. Just as Gasché deliberately ignores Derrida's devastating critique of Hegel, which is no less devastating for being mounted in a quasi-literary style (really a form of textual catachresis, as I discuss below), so he ignores the youthful remainders, the human refuse that Plato apparently didn't think about very much either. But Derrida's *Glas* is at the very least a significant challenge to the abstract philosophical discourse of the tradition. We continue to ignore it and the problems it highlights—and need it be said these are the very problems with which, as a society, we are most desperately trying to deal—at our own peril. Gasché's powerful analytical discourse demonstrates that to choose to ignore *Glas* is dangerously close to choosing to ignore the most vital issues of our time. This intersubjective violence operates at the level of text, to be sure, but there is also always a level of "writing" that is etched into real human lives, like the tattoo sessions the young Jean Genet witnesses at Mettray or the police baton blows administered to Rodney King.

Richard Rorty would offer his version of nominalism, or what he calls a Deweyian or Wittgensteinian pragmatism, as an alternative to Gasché's austerely analytical project, implying that these two alternatives nicely cover the field of possible inquiry into Derrida's work. As he says in conclusion to a recent essay, "Still, it may be of service to those coming to Derrida for the first time to have a choice between opposed readings at their disposal" ("Is Derrida a Transcendental Philosopher?" 128). Rorty mocks any Marxist use of the term *capitalism* as one of those heavy words that used to do service in a discourse but now look rather funny; yet his own use of the liberal vs. conservative reading of Derrida, in keeping with the values of liberal democracy he espouses, invokes the market-forces ideology underlying such a "choice." Rorty would undoubtedly deny that his discourse repeats any such gesture, which could be called, following my discussion of Derrida's analysis of writing in the *Grammatology,* intersubjective violence. In Rorty's self-described Wittgensteinian language games or nominalist philosophy, there is no clear link between the kind of games that philosophers perform with language and really existing states of affairs. (That he has misappropriated and misdescribed Wittgenstein is a topic for some further discussion.) Philosophers merely try to persuade other people using the various language strategies available to them. There are the rigorous, argumentative types, among whom Rorty classes Gasché, and the "world-disclosive" dreamers, among whom Rorty classes Heidegger and Derrida (123ff.). Gasché's problem, according to Rorty, is that he tries to make Derrida sound like a serious, argumentative philosopher, searching for bedrock truths, when in fact he is really a prankster, spinning humorous riffs on ideas from the philosophical tradition.

There are some things that Rorty says about Gasché with which I concur, including the idea that Gasché's talk of "infrastructures" makes claims for Derrida's use of terms like *trace* and *différance* that seem clearly out of keeping with Derrida's stated goals and aims (125ff.). My own criticism of Gasché, of course, is not that he is too serious and doesn't realize what a trickster Derrida really is, but that his discourse on Derrida moves onto such an abstract level that it leaves behind important ethical questions, and the means for addressing those questions, which Derrida, in my view, has been developing all along in his deconstructive thinking. Gasché's idealizing, or Hegelian, bias causes him to want to ask questions of a transcendental nature—which Rorty is correct in characterizing as foundational—seeking to find out how things truly are, or to establish a terminology that best corresponds to reality. This does not mean, however, that the only viable alternative is to reject all such language as necessarily flawed and turn instead to a radical relativist position. Derrida's writings on the *trace* and *différance* may not carry the argument-structure that Gasché wants to assign to them,[8] but that does not mean that the only other alternative is to view Derrida as a philosophical humorist with a fine sense of style (see Rorty, "Two Meanings of Logocentrism" 113).

I want to focus on a specific passage from Rorty's essay in which he again, in shorthand form, states some of the central arguments that he has developed in works such as *Contingency, Irony, and Solidarity* concerning the total dissociation of philosophical language games from real-life situations. In the language of this passage, there are moments when such a dissociation seems tenuous at best. Rorty says:

> Nominalists see language as just human beings using marks and noises to get what they want. One of the things we want to do with language is to get food, another is to get sex, another is to understand the origin of the universe. Another is to enhance our sense of human solidarity, and still another may be to create oneself by developing one's own private, autonomous, philosophical language. It is possible that a single vocabulary might serve two or more of these aims, but there is no reason to think that there is any great big meta-vocabulary which will somehow get at the least common denominator of all the various uses of all the various marks and noises which we use for all these various purposes. So there is no reason to lump these uses together into something big called "Language," and then to look for its "condition of possibility." ("Is Derrida a Transcendental Philosopher?" 127)

So, in Rorty's view, the idea that there might be some way of seeking common structures between different levels of language use—the "intersubjective violence" for example, that serves as a horizon for thinking the complexly interrelated structures that Derrida has termed "writing" —is classed together with idealist attempts such as Gasché's to find transcendental preconditions for our language and knowledge of the world, and thus rejected. Rorty argues instead that there is a radical disjunction between philosophical language—which can be so outlandish as to be a form of private expression (another misreading of Wittgenstein)—and the everyday language with which human beings go about getting their daily needs met. Rorty doesn't see much problem then with describing this latter, everyday level of activity, functionally sealed off from the language of philosophy, science, and political theory.

Maybe this attitude concerning an unproblematic description of everyday language leads Rorty to speak more quickly than he wants, or perhaps he would argue that in these few sentences he is dropping the specialized language of philosophy and temporarily adopting an everyday discourse; but in either case we need to ask how to account for the disturbing locution "get sex." This is, at the very least, an instance of what Luce Irigaray has called the *sexuation* of discourse, not because the content of the phrase concerns sex, but because the language used unmistakably identifies the speaker's gender. As Derrida said, famously, of Levinas (an instance I will be revisiting in the final chapter), this discourse could only have been produced by a man. As much feminist discourse has insisted, ways of speaking about sex and gender reveal deeply held attitudes, which are not for that reason to be seen as somehow "natural." The idea that sex is something that women *have* and that men try to *get* is part of what some women have called our "rape culture."[9] Men and women in our culture are not born with such attitudes toward sex; they are trained to have them. The presence of such attitudes, in turn, influences individuals' behavior, and much more, including, in this particular area, the way that rape is dealt with in the law enforcement and legal communities. The idea that men want to "get sex" is one step from the "natural man" argument that says men are entitled to act on their "natural" urges and that women do not have the right to say "no" past a certain point. This is clearly not to say that Rorty is a rapist, or that his discourse actively intends to promote such behaviors. The point is rather that there are *always* connections (often as not unintended) between one's language usages and actually existing states of affairs—even in a discourse, such as Rorty's, that would present itself as purely "philosophical." In my reading, one of the goals of Derrida's deconstructive endeavor has consistently been to insist on such connections. The intersubjective violence underlying language and all other sociocultural structures—law, economics, family, religion, and so forth—is what Derrida means to implicate in his widening of the term "writing" to refer catchrestically to these other phenomena shaping and shaped by human culture.

In a recent article, Sharon Marcus has developed a powerful argument that rape be viewed as "a linguistic fact." As she says: "Another way to refuse to recognize rape as the real fact of our lives is to treat it as a *linguistic* fact: to ask how the violence of rape is enabled by narratives, complexes and institutions which derive their strength not from outright, immutable, unbeatable force but rather from their power to structure our lives as imposing cultural scripts. To understand rape in this way is to understand it as subject to change" (388–89). Now, clearly someone like Marcus, who moves onto a level of analysis that utilizes writing in Derrida's expanded sense of the term, would reject Rorty's claim concerning the dissociation between language and how people conduct their lives. She further urges that it may be from deconstructing the "cultural script" that the most effective intervention may be made in this area. The question of whether such a deconstruction would have occurred absent the writings of Derrida is no doubt moot (if not insulting, which I do not mean to be), and Derrida is nowhere cited in Marcus's article. The connection is rather that Marcus develops a powerful argument concerning writing and language in a way, that, if understood, can only serve to refute such bland, quiescent versions of Derrida's philosophy, and of theory in general, as proposed by such thinkers as Rorty. Developing the notion of the cultural script, Marcus argues: "The rape script takes its form from what I will call a *gendered grammar of violence,* where grammar means the rules and structure which assign people to positions within a script" (392). The "rape script" is recognizably a language game in Wittgenstein's sense. Active, politically oriented interventions such as Marcus's that make use of postmodern theory show Rorty's brand of quiescent relativism to be fatally flawed—that is, both dangerous and doomed to irrelevance—as a way to view the world and as an interpretive model for Derrida, Wittgenstein, and others. My own intervention here, which risks trivializing Marcus's important contribution to the discussion of rape, should be seen as a way of insisting on the ethical significance of the deconstructive project, an ethical significance that is noticeably absent, for the most part, from either Gasché's or Rorty's discussion of Derrida.

Glas and Derrida's Post-*Glas* Itinerary

Derrida's *Glas*—despite appearances—may be his most serious attempt to confront the ethical issues that he first addressed in the *Grammatology,* that is, how to think "writing" in the large sense that he gives it as underlying and informing all of the sociosymbolic systems of human interrelations, culture, and exchange. If the horizon within which such an attempt to think writing is necessarily that of *intersubjective violence* (*Grammatology* [G], 127, 185), Derrida in *Glas* asks how the philosophical tradition of Hegel and others has faced this question, and whether their ethical thinking still holds for us. Yet, despite the seriousness of this enterprise, the critical response to *Glas*, at least in the English-language criticism, has for the most part concentrated on the writerly aspect of the text.[10] Just as Derrida is arguably utilizing a form of catachresis in his use of the term "writing" (and many other terms: *différance, trace, reste, parergon, cendre,* and so on), so *Glas* seems to be operating as a form of *textual catachresis,* where the appearance of the text itself on the page is being asked to serve new functions, take on new meanings, create a different space of textuality. But if that were *all* that the text of *Glas* was doing, it would be a weak effort indeed, deserving to be left out of any rigorous account of Derrida's philosophizing, as Gasché urges, and thus of interest primarily to those "playful" Derrideans like Hartman and Rorty. Clearly, one of the questions Derrida is raising through his use of the textual catachresis of *Glas* is: How does one begin to deal with the philosophers of the tradition? If one remains within the language of argument and demonstrative proofs, then one ends up with a discussion much like that of Gasché. If one takes the nominalist/pragmatist approach of someone like Rorty, one views the text of Hegel ironically, and ironic distance becomes part of the (humorous) discourse with which one discusses Hegel and others.

Derrida's textual catachresis attempts not one or the other of these approaches, but both, and then some. It is a sign of tentativeness on the part of the existing critical, theoretical, and philosophical discourses that *Glas* presents such difficulties for subsequent interpretation. Gasché represents a late idealist/Hegelian tradition, which while finding much in Derrida to delve into, yet dismisses *Glas* and other "playful" texts as unworthy of serious attention. Rorty, in his radical relativism, delights in the view of *Glas* as a humorous diversion for those with training in the philosophical tradition; he sees *Glas* as a text that helps to create an ironic distance between philosophizing and real-life situations, thus maintaining a certain space for the specialized philosophical endeavor of those Rorty views as being like himself. Jürgen Habermas criticizes the writerly dimension of texts like *Glas* for attempting to blur the boundary distinctions between philosophy and literature.[11] These alternately bland and hysterical responses to *Glas* indicate, from my perspective, both that the existing discourses are ill-prepared to accommodate the thinking such a text represents, and that Derrida must therefore be doing something right, something that presents an ongoing challenge for future thinking.

One such challenge to thinking is the way the two columns of *Glas* "talk" to each other (see my discussion in chapter 3). This becomes thematized at times in the text, as in "the infinite exchange of two columns which gaze backwards at each other [l'échange infini de deux colonnes qui se regardent à l'envers]" (53; trans. 43b modified). The intertwining of the two columns can be seen as a *chiasmus*: "X, almost perfect chiasmus [X, chiasme presque parfait]" (53b; trans. 43b modified). The thinking of the chiasmus maintains and deepens the reflections in the phenomenological tradition of Merleau-Ponty (see chapter 2). Merleau-Ponty's problem for thinking was the dependence of the body on world in the act of perception, and whether some sort of reciprocity necessarily was thereby implied, leading to his tantalizing notion of "the flesh of the world [la chair du monde]." Lacan picked up on Merleau-Ponty's chiasmic relation between self and world in what he called "the spectacle of the world [le spectacle du monde]," the sense that the subject has of being regarded by inanimate things. This point from which the subject is caught in the captivating gaze is represented for Lacan in such phenomena as mirrors and anamorphosis, and in some sense stands for the unrepresentable Real at the center of the subject's Imaginary projections. Derrida has established an extreme distance from the thinking of both Merleau-Ponty and Lacan.[12] And yet his own thinking on the chiasmus is embedded in both the phenomenological tradition of the former and the psychoanalytic nexus of the latter. By establishing a chiasmic relation between the columns dealing with Hegel and Genet, Derrida overlays his own intertextual strategies upon the phenomenological and psychoanalytic issues that are also clearly at play.

Hegel's discourse in *The Philosophy of Right* cannot attain to the level of purely reflective abstraction that Gasché claims for Hegel's project generally. Just as Gasché himself overlooks the strange, quasi-analogical links in his own discourse (as in the exclusion of the radically other in Plato's *symploke*, represented *in Plato's text* by the banishment or execution of the bad boys of Athens, an instance that Gasché fails even to remark), so Hegel's most important concepts rely on weird links that are at once metaphorical and nonmetaphorical.[13]

The Hegelian *Aufhebung*, for example (which thinkers like Gasché still invoke as what Rorty would call a magical word to perform a whole series of philosophical maneuvers), is explained in Hegel's text, as Derrida says, by "the relation of copulation and sexual difference" (*Glas* 127a; trans. 111a). This way of describing the lifting up, annulment, and preservation of conceptual differences is both analogical and strangely literal. Analogically, copulation explains the operation of *Aufhebung*, in showing how differences (in this case, gender differences) get together while remaining distinct and yet creating something new. Copulation as the sexual activity of husband and wife is also the literal link in marriage, which for Hegel is the founding moment of social morality, or *Sittlichkeit*. Now, one could argue with Hegel's choice of analogies, or one could question whether such analogies truly function as logical steps, or one could simply dismiss Hegel as an outdated representative of a certain brand of patriarchal thinking. But to engage in these arguments one would have to use the language of argument that is marked by such concepts as *Aufhebung* and *Sittlichkeit*, or, as Derrida said often in his early works, one would have to use the language of metaphysics.

In Derrida's textual catachresis in *Glas*, however, the Genet column comments in chiasmic fashion on Hegel's weird choice of analogy. Why is Hegel's choice of copulation to symbolize the *Aufhebung* strange? Well, for one thing, it normativizes heterosexual intercourse, leaving nonheterosexuals like Jean Genet forever on the "outside."[14] But, beyond even that exclusionary move, Genet presents a living, actual example of someone who fell through the cracks of the social morality (*Sittlichkeit*) centered on the institution of marriage—since he was abandoned shortly after birth by his presumably unmarried mother. As the Genet column of *Glas* says repeatedly: "*Reste—la mère* [Remains—the mother]" (132b; trans. 115b). One could make the normative psychoanalyzing connection and infer that Genet's abandonment by his mother *caused* him to become homosexual, but that would likewise miss the point (not merely irrelevant, but probably just wrong). The case of Genet demonstrates that Hegel's logic of the family as anchoring social morality is bound to leave something—and, not incidentally, lots of little someones—out of the picture. Such is the *reste*, the remainder, that which remains after the universalizing philosopher has supposedly accounted for everything that really matters.[15] Now, if we don't care much about orphans raised by the state (or drug users or the unemployed or homeless people or people who are HIV-positive), then this may seem unimportant. But Genet's example also shows that society's "orphans" sometimes grow up not only to challenge the logic of the society that produced them, but, at the same time, to justify and even to celebrate those same logics. The "radical exteriority" of Jean Genet's texts is thus both "outside" and "inside" the foundational narratives of culture.

Just as Hegel, in Derrida's analysis, founds social morality on the instance of the family, so he founds the ultimate legitimation of the law, and thus of individual freedom, on the death penalty.[16] Strangely enough, so does Jean Genet. But from Genet's "inverted" perspective, execution by the state is the quasi-religious experience that gives meaning to the whole existence of the imprisoned criminal population: "la mort sur l'échafaud qui est notre gloire [the death on the scaffold which is our glory]" (MR 4). Those beings who are sentenced to death have a "sacred" quality that illumines the lives of the other inmates.[17] Lou-du-point-du-jour (Lou Daybreak) meets Jeannot and a friend the moment after the supreme criminal Harcamone has been executed, a moment that Genet describes: "Il était campé haut, les mains sur son ventre. Pour nous, pour Divers et moi, il était la personnification du moment fatidique, il était l'aube, le point du jour. Jamais jusqu'alors son nom n'avait eu si exacte signification [He was standing erect, with hands on his stomach. To us, to Divers and me, he was the personification of the fateful moment. He was dawn, daybreak. Never before had his name been so meaningful]" (MR 371; trans. 282). A law founded on capital punishment, following out the logic from the "other" side, leads to just such a glorification of the condemned, which is both metaphorical and not. The point being that Genet is not only up to the task of thinking through such issues as the foundation of the law and the significance of the family to "normal" morality; his own logic is the mirror image, the chiasmic reflection, of Hegel's philosophical system. The *reste*, or remainder, left outside the social system, left to dangle in a conceptual nonspace by Plato and Hegel alike, strangely, uncannily, returns to demonstrate the inescapability of certain kinds of logical moves that philosophers of the tradition have proposed. But Genet, in his way, is also more honest in his account, in that he does not overlook or deny the underlying, systemic violence that such a logic both generates and depends upon.

Now, one could say that Derrida wants to blur the boundary between philosophy and literature by juxtaposing these analyses of Hegel and Genet, but that would be to remain within a kind of limiting logic that as much as anything else Derrida wants both to point out and, in some sense, leave behind.[18] As he proposes in "The Law of Genre," for example, "a text would not *belong* to any genre. Every text *participates* in one or several genres, there is no genreless text, there is always a genre and genres, yet such participation never amounts to a belonging" (264; AL 230).[19] What he thus terms a "participation without belonging [participation sans appartenance]" (256; AL 227; italics in the original) constitutes a way of confronting those difficulties of thinking—such as the substantializing of concepts—in the philosophical-literary discourse that he has been dealing with at least since the *Grammatology.* Another way to say this is that the texts of literature or philosophy are not simply "*interior* to" those discourses.[20] Genet's text inverts and mirrors the logic of Hegel, producing moving meditations on love, family, sexuality, and mortality that fall "outside" the philosopher's totalizing system. In his coherent mirroring of these topics, however, Genet shows the persistence of certain unthinkable mysteries. That these same mysteries can be shown to motivate literary efforts is a threat only to those who want to claim that philosophy has a privileged claim to think even what cannot be thought.

The issues at work in *Glas* are also at work in Derrida's other texts from this period. The *reste* of *Glas* is demonstrably working in the same area as other Derridean terms such as *trace* and *restance*, for example. Having already examined, to some extent, the links between the *Grammatology* and *Glas* (linking the "early" Derrida to this transitional work from 1974), it may be important to discuss briefly some of the nonobvious links between Derrida's ethical philosophy in *Glas* and another text from the seventies. One would not think that the essay "Signature événement contexte" (M 365–93; trans. 1–23) would have led to far-reaching discussions of ethical issues, but perhaps by examining the links between the term *reste* as used in *Glas* and the *restance* (translated eventually as "remainder") Derrida proposes in the translation, "Signature Event Context [SEC]," some of the reasons for this ethical debate may become more evident.

The term *restance,* theorized in SEC, is a development of the term *trace* that Derrida claims is a generalizable structure of all "writing" in the catachrestic sense developed in the *Grammatology.* In SEC, Derrida is arguing, for one thing, that the same structure of the functioning of the sign is applicable to both the written and spoken utterance. One element of this structure is that the sign has a certain meaning, and even a kind of existence, in the absence of speaker, hearer, or referent, and that it is the very possibility—insistence, persistence, falling away—of such a meaning that makes the sign a sign at all. This leads him to say: "This structural possibility of being separated from the referent or from the signified (hence from communication and from its context) seems to me to make every mark, including those which are oral, a grapheme in general; which is to say, as we have seen, the nonpresent *remainder* [*restance*] of a differential mark cut off from its putative 'production' or origin. And I shall extend this law to all 'experience' in general if it is conceded that there is no experience consisting of *pure* presence but only of chains of differential marks" (SEC 10; modified).[21] This passage contains in capsule form many of Derrida's themes, and one would not expect critics who are unsympathetic to his project to acquiesce to all of the "givens" that he here adduces, particularly the way he seems to erase the everyday notion of experience. Yet in John Searle's famous response to Derrida, he picks out the notion of *restance* to criticize (200). This allows Derrida, in "Limited Inc a b c," to clarify what is at stake in the use of the term *restance*. Far from being the "permanence" of the written sign, which Searle interprets it as, *restance* is what is in some sense *never there at all*, but yet occupies what Derrida insists is the productive position of allowing for the mark to come into being (*Limited Inc* 50–54). Derrida says he will *not* link this discussion of *restance* to his discussion elsewhere of the *reste* (52), but if one were to do just this, something of the ethical import of the term might be that much more salient.

Derrida has struggled to insist that deconstruction is not a form of "negative theology" or negative ontology. His discussion of *restance* in SEC is part of the explanation of "iterability" in speech acts.[22] That signs have meaning in the possible absence of sender, receiver, and referent, that this possibility is what makes them signs in the first place, leads to the necessary possibility of citation, grafting, and parody. By trying to isolate the serious from the nonserious, speech act theory has to marginalize these various "literary" functionings of language. One of Derrida's "points" in putting forth the notion of iterability is that these very literary possibilities, although we might want to exclude them from discussion, are radically at the center of the sign-structure. In ontological terms, one could say that the death or absence of the speaker is already implied in the use of the sign *qua* sign; the possibility of the sign's being repeated, either in its "proper" sense or in a parodic or literary usage haunts the sign in what could be called, staying within a certain language of the philosophical tradition, its "condition of possibility."[23] The issue of exclusion that Derrida alludes to while not invoking it in "Limited Inc a b c" is a way of examining the ethical aspect of this problematic. If our philosophizing of speech acts is to be founded on notions like "everyday language," "normal usage," and "intersubjectively shared meanings," what is the cost in terms of the excluded other, the other that is always *there* structurally in the first place. *Restance* is translated by "remainder," which could equally well translate *reste*. It is theoretically possible to discuss language use in terms that do not specifically invoke ethical issues, but that does not therefore mean these issues are absent from the discussion. *Contra* Rorty, language and writing form a continuum inseparable from everyday life (not only, or even primarily, because language invokes the referential function, as Robert Scholes argues in his attempt to refute deconstruction), and part of Derrida's ongoing project is to show how these links function, both at the microlinguistic level (*restance*) and at the level of social theory (*reste*). The force of Derrida's thinking derives at least in part from showing that we separate these levels at our peril.

The "Impossibility" of Deconstruction

One problem with using terminology like "conditions of possibility" to describe Derrida's deconstructive project (see Gasché and Harvey) is that it is by no means certain that deconstruction is even possible. This impossibility of deconstruction may seem to point to the related ideas of "aporia" and "undecidability," terms that have become fashionable in the proliferating discourses of literary deconstruction, where they are often invoked to support a radical relativism or lack of epistemic foundation; but another view is that deconstruction's impossibility is one way of describing deconstruction as an ethical practice.[24] As Derrida says in "Psyché," an essay in which he treats the work of his friend Paul de Man: "For a deconstructive operation *possibility* would rather be the danger, the danger of becoming an available set of rule-governed procedures, methods, accessible approaches. The interest of deconstruction, of such force and desire as it may have, is a certain experience of the impossible: that is . . . of the other—the experience of the other as the invention of the impossible, in other words, as the only possible invention" (AL 328).[25] Derrida invokes here the subtitle of the essay, "Invention of the Other," a nod toward the difficult task of describing the complicated thought of someone like Paul de Man, but also a move in the direction of the ethical discourse of Emmanuel Levinas. By referring to a "set of rule-governed procedures," Derrida might seem to be offering a mild rebuke to American-style deconstructors, but this kind of language is also in keeping with ways of describing normative ethical standards. As we shall see, "impossibility" develops increasingly strong resonances in Derrida's recent writings, especially as he attempts to take on ethical issues.

Robert Bernasconi has explored the link between Derrida's and Levinas's ethical thinking in a powerful essay, "Deconstruction and the Possibility of Ethics." While I do not fully agree with Bernasconi's contention that Derrida's early essay "Violence and Metaphysics" moves all the way in the direction of Levinas's ethical thinking, I agree fully with Bernasconi's development of the subsequent steps that bring Derrida and Levinas into close proximity on these issues. Bernasconi says, strongly: "The demand that deconstruction provide *an* ethics betrays not only traditional presuppositions about the possibility of generating ethical systems, but also a miscomprehension about the nature of deconstruction, confusing it for one philosophy among others. Hence in the face of the demand for an ethics, deconstruction can reply, in the course of its reading of Levinas that *the ethical relation is impossible and 'the impossible has already occurred' at this very moment*" (135; italics in the original). In my reading of Bernasconi's argument, the ethical relation itself is impossible because it precedes the constitution of the subject as the radically other to which the subject is always called upon to respond, in the thinking of Levinas. Levinas's ethics as what he calls the "first philosophy" (see chapter 4) means that the full extent of the subject's involvement in the web of other-directed relationships always escapes the grasp of rational explanation or control. The italicized phrase, *"the impossible has already occurred,"* from Derrida's later essay on Levinas, "En ce moment même," paradoxically answers or fulfills the ethical demand that reason has declared to be impossible.

"Of that which one cannot speak," Wittgenstein says famously in the *Tractatus*, "one must remain silent" (§7). Derrida rewrites this in his "Envois" as: "That which one cannot say, one must by all means not keep silent, but write it [Ce qu'on ne peut pas dire, il ne faut surtout pas taire, mais l'écrire]" (CP 209; trans. 194 modified). Those who wish to maintain the seriousness of Derrida's philosophical project might wish to look away from utterances like this, but in my view Derrida has maintained all along that there cannot be any strict separation between the serious and the nonserious (see *Limited Inc*). Derrida's insistence on the impossibility of certain kinds of discourse leads, not to the rejection of what is at stake in them, but toward a serious examination of the presuppositions surrounding their expression. Another way of approaching this question is Derrida's thinking on the gift. Throughout his texts, he has been promising for some time to make a major statement on the gift. In a strange way, it is part of his thinking on the gift that his giving forth of it should be both promised and deferred; in Derrida's thinking the gift recedes (infinitely) from the reader's grasp.[26] In "En ce moment même," for example, Derrida says: "The gift *is not*. One cannot ask 'what is the gift?'; yet it is only on that *condition* that there will have been, by this name or another, a gift" (*Psyché* 163; trans. 15).[27] Not only can one not ask what the gift is, or where it comes from; once there is a gift, one cannot hold onto it. Or, as Derrida says in "Envois," "no gift without absolute forgetting [pas de don sans oubli absolu]" (CP 181; trans. 167 modified). The radical forgetting of the gift means in one sense that it cannot become the "norm" for subsequent ethical behavior or decisions. This "singularity" of the gift in turn relates it to Derrida's thinking on the *reste*, *restance*, and iterability.[28]

The gift is a way of preparing the arrival of the other, and thus we might call it an attitude (what Rimbaud called an "ardent patience"). But it is also a practice, linked in Derrida, as it is in the work of Hélène Cixous, with reading and writing (see Cixous, *Entre l'écriture*). The gift is the affirmative side of Derrida's activity that he refers to as deconstruction. Deconstruction is patient, attentive, rigorous, open-ended. Deconstruction allows for the "coming to writing" of Cixous's formulation; it is also a way of preparing the "coming of the other" in Derrida's thinking. He says, in the essay "Psyché": "The invention of the other, coming of the other, this is not *constructed* certainly as a subjective genitive, nor as an objective genitive, even if the invention comes from the other. Because this one here, from then on, is neither subject nor object, not an I, nor a consciousness, nor an unconscious. *To prepare oneself for that coming of the other, this is what one could call deconstruction"* (*Psyché* 53; my italics).[29] This attitude of patient attentiveness, preparing the way for the arrival of the other, is the aspect of deconstruction I have been calling ethical. The hesitation and qualification Derrida employs in his descriptions of deconstruction, especially in its ethical aspect, are necessary to say first what ethics is *not,* or not to say what ethics *is* or *should be.* Ethics in the philosophical tradition is usually seen as answering the questions: What should one do? or, How should one live? The various answers proposed by philosophy and religious practices generally take the form of prescriptive phrases, or alternatively, outline the general form for such phrases.[30] At least since Nietzsche, philosophers have been more hesitant to embrace such prescriptions, which can be seen as the legitimation of regimes of power and intersubjective domination (as discussed in my introduction). The deconstructive task then is to find ways of describing a nonnormative or nonprescriptive ethics, an ethics that maintains an openness to the other as truly other, not merely an other who is the "same," following the analogy of universal humanism.[31]

In the Levinasian strain of ethical thinking that both Simon Critchley and Robert Bernasconi have identified in Derrida's work, this task for deconstructive thinking is profoundly linked to the possibility, or impossibility, of philosophy generally. Here is Critchley, forcefully outlining this conclusion: "For both Levinasian ethics and Derridian deconstruction, this 'infrastructural' matrix of alterity would try to show the conditions under which something like logocentrism or ontology is possible, whilst at the same time showing how the philosophical pretension or ontological totality is continually rendered impossible by an alterity that can neither be reduced nor excluded. *Derrida and Levinas seek the conditions for the possibility and impossibility of philosophical conceptuality"* ("The Chiasmus" 103–4; italics in the original). Critchley's statement moves well to outline the question of deconstruction's "impossibility" and what this means, both in the lineations of the contexts from which it stems and in the radical alterity that at all times challenges philosophy's self-transparency. The emphasis placed on the radical alterity that challenges philosophy's totalizing project recalls the previous discussion of *Glas* and the inherent instability of any project that would found an ethical system based on exclusionary or normative rules.

The "impossibility" of deconstruction, from this perspective, means that deconstruction can never become a set of self-transparent rules for thinking or conduct, but the challenge it poses to thinking and conduct nonetheless maintains the force of an ethical demand. To see why this is so means revisiting the relationship of Derrida's thinking to Levinas's ethical philosophy, in the context of Derrida's more recent essay, "En ce moment même." The singularity of language and forms of address in this essay in turn lead to an examination of other recent texts that together may be said to comprise Derrida's "negative" autobiography.

Chapter Seven

Derrida's "Negative" Autobiography

The "impossibility" of deconstruction leads to the formulation regarding its ethical aspect that it seems necessary to say first what ethics is not, or, alternatively, *not to say* what ethics is or should be. Since the ethical demand, in the sense that Derrida continues to develop out of Levinas's philosophy, is always in some sense prior, the nonnormative formulation of an ethical response must take the form of a singularity (see Altieri, "Frank Stella and Jacques Derrida" 171). Derrida has recently been exploring a textual practice that situates the utterance strongly in a specific context as a means of highlighting this singularity. This move continues the textual practice that is so prominent in *Glas* (as examined in the previous chapter), increasingly through exploring the "auto" of autobiography, situating the *grapheme* in a kind of fragmented—or what I will be refering to as a "negative"—autobiography. Critics are understandably divided on the meaning of this move to what in any other writer would be called the personal dimension. Is this a means of exploring certain kinds of political issues not possible even in the extremely inventive textual practice of texts such as *Glas*? Or is this rather an interiorizing move that denies those political implications that arise from contextualizing writing as a form of "intersubjective violence"? These questions recall those raised previously: What is intersubjective violence? and, Is the practice of ethical deconstruction even possible? The violence of one's encounters with the texts of others necessarily involves these questions, wherein the personal is necessarily intersubjective and "impossibility" paradoxically provides a means of assuming critical responsibility. Situating these textual encounters in an autobiographical context removes any possibility of logocentric abstraction that would render such responsibility prescriptive in terms of a normative ethics. Rather, the singular site of the writing ensures that the ethical demand is impossible and "*the impossible has already occurred.*"

Derrida's "Negative" Autobiography

Derrida's move to an increasingly personal discourse certainly upsets the dogmatic reception of his work that operates along the lines of the speech/writing binary.[1] In the "Envois" of *La carte postale,* Derrida wittily rewrites the end of Wittgenstein's *Tractatus:* "That which one cannot say, one must by all means not keep silent, but write it" (CP 209; trans. 194 modified). The "Envois" themselves are a text of an unrepeatable singularity based on the premise of a writer much like Derrida writing to an absent loved one. The first publication of *Feu la cendre* (*Cinders*) was issued simultaneously by the press *des femmes* with a cassette of Derrida reading the text with French actress Carole Bouquet, and the text itself refers to this question of voice and oral presentation (see *Cinders* 23). These moves, along with the increasingly autobiographical tenor of the essays published in the same time period, lend support to Derrida's repeated claim that his work does not attempt to establish the dominance of writing in the speech/writing complex, but rather to point out the limitations of logocentrically based philosophy. *Feu la cendre* is a very personal text that investigates, among other issues, the debt due to others in one's own writing and intellectual pursuits. This debt is "unspeakable" for reasons that emerge from one's own singular personal context, but merge and interact with a whole complex of philsophical issues, including prominently the ethical demand.

How one can *not* speak of these things, or "How to avoid speaking [*Comment ne pas parler*]," is a question Derrida interrogates in an essay of that title (*Psyché* 535–95; trans. DNT 73–142). This essay takes as its subject negative theology, an area of philosophical inquiry with which Derrida has often been associated because of a common critical view of the negative capacity of the deconstructive strategy. As he says in the essay, however, this is paradoxically an area he had never consciously attempted, for complex reasons, some of them autobiographical, to study. This idea of being somehow forced, or backed in, to talking about the topic leads to a startling autobiographical turn. In the essay he says, in a cryptic footnote, that this is his most autobiographical essay, because he is *not* talking about important areas of his personal experience.

He confines himself in this essay to thinking the tradition of negative theology in the Greek and Christian contexts, leaving out those of Jewish and Muslim thought. Derrida explains this decision:

> Despite this silence, or in fact because of it, one will perhaps permit me to interpret this lecture as the most "autobiographical" speech I have ever risked. One will attach to this word as many quotation marks as possible. It is necessary to surround with precautions the hypothesis of a self-presentation passing through a speech on the negative theology of others. But if one day I had to tell my story, nothing in this narrative would start to speak of the thing itself if I did not come up against this fact; for lack of capacity, competence or self-authorization, I have never yet been able to speak of what my birth, as one says, should have made closest to me: the Jew, the Arab.
>
> This small piece of autobiography confirms it obliquely. It is performed in all of my foreign languages: French, English, German, Greek, Latin, the philosophic, metaphilosophic, Christian, etc.
>
> In brief: how not to speak of oneself? But also: how to do it without allowing oneself be invented by the other? or without inventing the other? (*Psyché* 562n; trans. DNT 135–36n)

This statement also yields a different angle on how the activity of deconstruction produces a discourse, in addition to the widely discussed "double reading" that he had proposed early on in the *Grammatology*. Impossibility weighs heavily on this utterance, producing resonances with many of the themes we have been examining until this point. But new questions are raised in this context as well. What exactly is "the invention of the other"? And what is Derrida's relation to his Jewish background?

In many ways, the most personal response to the question of his Jewish background is to be found in his "Circonfession." In this text, Derrida writes around several questions, basing his investigation on the text of St. Augustine's *Confessions*. This strategy allows Derrida to refer, sometimes directly and sometimes obliquely, to the North African background he shares with this Christian father. One of the main ways Derrida invokes this comparison is through Augustine's references to his mother. Whereas in the "Envois" the privileged interlocutor is in some sense imaginary, elided or made up of compound figures, the address to the mother in "Circonfession" is very direct and personal. As the title of the piece suggests, Derrida combines his ruminations on the Augustinian confession with his own reflections on the act and significance of ritual circumcision. Section 10 recounts his being called to Nice to attend to his mother in the hospital, expecting her to die, and seeing her pull through, with references to St. Augustine's parallel experience, ending: "and I write between two resurrections, one that is given then the one that is promised, compromised to this almost natural monument which becomes in my eyes a sort of calcinated root, the naked spectacle of a photographed wound—the scab cauterized by the light of writing, to fire, to blood but also to ashes" (54–55; trans. 54 modified). Circumcision, referred to earlier in the passage, links with the themes throughout Derrida's writing—trace, difference, parergon, cinder—as the absent or scarred trace of something else, a kind of writing of or on the body that merges here with the body of the mother, who in turn, like circumcision, is one of Derrida's links to the traditions of Judaism. This highly personal response becomes a singular site, as one's own circumcised penis is always in some sense singular, as is one's relationship to one's mother. Such a singularity both does and doesn't obey the laws of iteration, in that ritual circumcision is performed according to the sacred rites, in ways that are significantly related to textual practices, but each time is nevertheless at least somewhat contingent on circumstances. One sign of this contingency is some oblique references to Derrida's own sons perhaps not being circumcised—and what does this say about Derrida's own role as a link (or not) in the tradition?

Returning to the essay on Levinas, "En ce moment même dans cet ouvrage me voici," allows an examination of these questions in the context of a discourse written in response to a prominent representative of the Jewish philosophical tradition, a philosopher so much a percursor of Derrida's own thought as to become almost familial. But for reasons not all that different from the personal address to the mother, the texture of this discourse is also affected by the unsaid, the unsayable.[2] It seems that Derrida is reticent to deal with the work of Levinas (perhaps because of the "violence" of his early essay?) and this reticence results in a text that is a virtual tissue of quotations from Levinas's work. Each phrase of the essay's title, as it turns out, is an encapsulation of significant stretches of analysis of the same phrase as it is used in Levinas's writings. To take but one example, the "ce moment" (this moment) is not an unproblematic phrase, because in the context of the ethical situation of being called by the other, that call has "always already" taken place. "This moment" takes place only in a web of temporality that is also a web of ethical responsibility. Speaking of the ethical obligation that always in some sense conditions the moment in question, Derrida says: "It follows that the responsibility in question is not merely said, named, thematized, in one or other occurrence of 'this moment,' it is first of all yours [*la tienne*], the one of reading to which 'this moment' is given, confided, or delivered over. Your reading is thus no longer merely a simple reading that deciphers the sense of what is already found in the text; it has a limitless (ethical) initiative [Ta lecture n'est donc plus une simple lecture déchiffrant le sens de ce qui se trouve déjà dans le texte, elle a une initiative (éthique) sans limite]" (*Psyché* 176; trans. 25). The moment of shock is registered in this passage by the untranslatable, familiar *you* (*tu*), with which Derrida establishes an intimate relation both to the reader and to the thinking of his philosophical colleague. This is the *you* (*tu*) that is a strong moment in Levinas's philosophy, the vocable by which the subject is called by the other: called, identified, called to account (as in the *I/Thou* of Buber's thinking). But because this *you* (*tu*) occurs in Derrida's close reading of the Levinasian text, the form of address is not merely theoretical, but highly personal, indicating Derrida's feeling of closeness, of indebtedness, to the thought of Levinas. In its grammatical forms then, the text *enacts* what it is talking about, and that is the limitless ethical obligation to the other implicated in any act of respectful reading and interpretation. This is one reason why this later essay appears to be a correction, even a retraction of the earlier "Violence and Metaphysics," and thus carries the kind of autobiographical weight that was suggested in "How to avoid speaking."[3]

Another strange moment in the later essay is provoked by Derrida's revisiting the theme of the *sexuation* of Levinas's discourse. He is commenting on his earlier assertion, in "Violence and Metaphysics," that Levinas's *Totality and Infinity* could only have been written by a man (cf. ED 228): "To himself, his text marks its signature by a masculine 'I-he,' a strange matter as was elsewhere noted 'in passing,' a while back, by an other [Son texte, à lui, marque sa signature d'un 'je-il' masculin, chose rare, cela fut noté ailleurs, 'au passage,' il y a longtemps, par un autre]" (*Psyché* 193; trans. 40). The irony of this passage is not limited to Derrida's self-description as "an other," but extends to the element of time (as much as twenty years) that has intervened

between his production of these different texts. He seems to be viewing his previous self with a humorous disdain, as though to say, How
could this young fellow have been so presumptuous? And yet (and yet),
the issue that young fellow raised so long ago has turned out not only
to have been startlingly prescient in terms of the entire range of subsequent feminist response to Levinas and others in the philosophical
tradition (especially the work of Irigaray), but Derrida's own text production has been drawn to experimentation with gendered markers for
the speaker, as when Derrida says in this essay, oddly (and parenthet-
ically): "I speak from my place as woman [je parle depuis ma place de
femme]" (*Psyché* 198; trans. 44). Now, there is no question that this is a
tricky gambit, but the issue of speaking as a woman does seem to
relate in turn to Derrida's negative autobiography, to the "invention of
the other," and to the impossibility of deconstruction.[4]

From crypt to ashes . . .

*Une trace a eu lieu. . . . même si elle **n'arrive qu'à s'effacer**, si
elle n'advient qu'en s'effaçant, l'effacement aura eu lieu, fût-il de
cendre. Il y a là cendre.*

A trace has taken place. . . . even if it *occurs only to efface itself,*
if it arises only in effacing itself, the effacement will have taken
place, even if its place is only in the ashes. *Il y a là cendre.*

("Comment ne pas parler" *Psyché* 560–61;
"How to avoid speaking" 98)

How to avoid speaking? What is the presence of the past that weighs
on the utterance? How to speak of that which is unspeakable?

What does it mean for an utterance to be cryptic?

What is the relation of crypt to ashes?

I want to claim that these are also aspects of Derrida's "negative"
autobiography. He says that the phrase *il y a là cendre* (*cinders there
are*) "came to me" (*Cinders* 21). He first placed it in a dedicatory statement at the end of *La dissémination*, explaining thereby—yet with a
maximum of "indirection"—the development of his thinking, the un-
payable debt owed to others, the traces of conversations and shared
ideas that can only be hinted at, never entirely remembered, because
that would be to interiorize what is first and most importantly an
exteriority. Like the terms *différance, trace, reste,* and so on, *cendre* is
being used catachrestically to point to something that cannot quite be

said. As such, we might say that *Feu la cendre* (*Cinders*) presents the text of an "unwritten" autobiography. At the very least there is the trace of an itinerary, the marks left in written texts by the phrase, whatever it means or doesn't mean, whatever it tries not to say while saying.

In *La dissémination*, Derrida explores the works of Philippe Sollers (especially *Nombres*), through a cross-tissue of extended quotations, much as he does with Levinas in "En ce moment même." He says, for example: "these *Numbers* tirelessly extract themselves from the crypt where you would have thought them ensconced. They remain undecipherable precisely because it is only in your representation that they ever took on the aplomb of a cryptogram hiding inside itself the secret of some meaning or reference" (402; trans. 362).[5] Derrida is here exploring some of the same territory as in his more abstract discussion of *restance* in SEC, the relation between writing and death. Why should the text of Sollers be like something extracted from a crypt? What a gothic notion, unless, of course, *crypt* is also taking on a catachrestic sense. The writing of *Nombres* is said to be undecipherable precisely because it exists only in the representation of the reader. But, even then, that representation depends on the writing taking on the allure of a cryptogram. We want to believe that there is some hidden sense or reference motivating the writing; this desire on the part of readers is therefore an unavoidable motivation of the sign, especially the hyperliterary sign in a text like that of Sollers.

What exactly is a cryptogram? In the essay, "La pharmacie de Platon," Derrida proposes some more (cryptic) explanation of this phenomenon: "If writing does belong to the *phusis*, wouldn't it be to that moment of the *phusis*, to that necessary movement through which its truth, the production of its appearing, tends, says Heraclitus, to take shelter in its crypt? 'Cryptogram' thus condenses in a single word the proposition of a pleonasm" (*La dissémination* 119; trans. 105 modified).[6] Cryptogram would be a pleonasm because each of its two parts means the "same" thing. Crypt, from this perspective, is always related to—even a synonym for—the *grammé*, writing as death: the carrier, the bearer of death.[7]

Crypt, of course, also bears meaning in the psychoanalytical discourse, a meaning that Derrida has explored in his foreword, "Fors," to a text by Nicolas Abraham and Maria Torok, *La cryptonymie: Le ver-*

bier de l'homme aux loups. In this foreword Derrida is paying a sort of homage to the work of Abraham, but he is also writing around the notion of crypt, which had occupied, as we have seen, a place in his discourse previously. The text by Abraham and Torok concerns the "private" language of Freud's Wolf Man; Derrida uses this text as a pretext to spin his own riffs on the psychoanalytic discourse, as well as his "theory" of writing.

The notion of crypt develops from the related Freudian concepts of identification, introjection, and incorporation. Whereas identification and introjection are the "normal" or normative means of developing one's identity in relation to others, incorporation relates to the inability to mourn that Freud claimed to discover in his treatment of hysteria.[8] The subject who incorporates the beloved/hated other takes the other in whole, rather than as an identificatory image, a kind of psychic cannibalism (although not that far removed from actual cannibalism, as seen in the chapter on Kristeva and her theories of abjection).[9] The incorporated other occupies the space of the crypt, from where he/she exerts an uncanny influence on the subject's behavior, but without, however, rising to the level of signification. This interior psychic space of crypt would be similar to Lacan's analysis of the Real (examined in chapter 4), and as opposed to introjection which, as Derrida puts it, "speaks": "incorporation keeps still, speaks only to silence or to ward off intruders from its secret place" ("Fors" 18; trans. xvii).

The space of the crypt leads to a secret language, relating to the verb *to encrypt,* or *to encode,* the adjective *cryptic* when applied to utterances. The Wolf Man's secret code makes extensive use of English words, as Abraham and Torok's exhaustive analysis shows. What is fascinating is that the secret code is the cryptic language of an unspeakable psychic situation, a relation to an other that cannot be avowed on the level of "everyday" language. As Derrida says, "To crypt: I do not think I have yet used it as a verb. To crypt is to cipher, a symbolic or semiotic operation that consists of manipulating a secret code, which is something one can never do alone" ("Fors" 53; trans. xxxvi).[10] The space of the crypt, then, is the result of the other being denied and yet maintained through the act of incorporation, a failed act of mourning. Its effect on the subject's language is to render it cryptic.

The cryptic language of philosophical utterances, and often poetry, thus might be said to bear this psychoanalytic dimension, which is also and always, of course, a social relation. The secret language of cryptic utterance is one way to separate one's listeners into the initiated and the uninitiated. The language of religious mysticism has often been shown to share many features with the language of the hysterical subject.[11] In Derrida's reading of Kant's pamphlet on apocalyptic thinking, "D'un ton apocalyptique adopté naguère en philosophie," this becomes an issue for establishing the difference between enlightenment thinking and mystical, or apocalyptic, thinking. Those who would announce the impending apocalypse are not only announcing the end of the world; they are also claiming to unveil thereby the ultimate truth, in the etymological sense of the word *apokalyptô* as unveiling (see Derrida, "D'un ton apocalyptique"). But when the revelation itself is announced in a cryptic language, necessarily designed to separate the initiate from the outsider and moreover to create a bond among members of the in-group, how does one determine between the unveiling and the veiling of truth? The religious or mystical leader claims this position of authority by simultaneously veiling and unveiling the truth. Derrida explains Kant's reading of this phenomenon as follows: "This *agogic* function of the leader of men, of *duce*, of *Führer*, of *leader* places him above the crowd he manipulates through the intermediary of *a small number of followers gathered into a sect with a crypted language*, a band, a clique or a small party with its ritualized practices" ("D'un ton" 451; trans. 128; final italics mine).[12] This would seem to be a fairly straightforward way to separate reason from unreason, mystical language from the language of enlightenment, and it would of course be Kant's position that such a separation is a fundamental necessity to rational social discourse. And yet, as Derrida notes: "Each of us is the mystagogue *and* the *Aufklärer* [enlightener] of an other [Chacun de nous est le mystagogue *et l'Aufklärer* d'un autre]" (462; trans. 142). This difficulty in distinguishing clearly between an enlightening and a mystifying discourse might seem to lend justification to Derrida's accusers, like Habermas, but we must also acknowledge the continuity in thinking between Derrida's version of undecidability in this essay and elsewhere in his work.

To get from crypt to ashes, we need to examine the analysis that Derrida performs on Heidegger's thinking on *Geist* (spirit or mind) and its appearance in Heidegger's "late" thinking as *Flamme* (flame).[13] This is also part of Derrida's spiritual, or "negative," autobiography, as he attempts to relate his interest in apocalyptic thinking with the history of the twentieth century. The purpose of Derrida's inquiry is not to scapegoat Heidegger, but rather to show that the rise of Nazi ideology is inextricable from the history of philosophy.[14] The greatest danger to one's current thinking on these issues may be to think that one can confidently identify *the other* as bearing the responsibility for the Nazi horror and, in so doing, innoculate oneself from any contagion.[15] If Heidegger's thinking contributed in whatever way to Nazi ideology, that thinking shows the entire tradition of philosophy to be what is at stake, and any totalizing, exclusionary system of thinking one might be tempted to engage in as well.[16] It is testament to the ethical character of Derrida's thinking that he is willing to engage in this close analysis of his important philosophical precursor—without at the same time trying to disenculpate himself.

Derrida's *De l'esprit* is a patient, rigorous, attentive, deconstructive reading of Heidegger's thinking on *Geist*, usually translated as spirit. Derrida shows that Heidegger himself stated the need to avoid this term, which weighs heavy in the German philosophical tradition. *Geist* in Heidegger's works leading up to *Being and Time* (1928) is seen as one of those terms on the side of Being—as opposed to the thing—which as yet cannot be apprehended in the Cartesian philosophy tradition leading into German idealism (HQ 28–29). Rather than trying to see the "substance" of human being as a synthesis between a body and a spirit, Heidegger urges a view of human being as *existence* (*Being and Time* §25; HQ 33). Derrida traces through *Being and Time* how Heidegger goes from not using the term *Geist* to using it in quotation marks, much like the speech-act distinction (which Derrida has repeatedly insisted is no distinction) between *usage* and *mention* (HQ 43; terms in English in the original). The point at which Heidegger embraces Nazism to the fullest extent is in his "Rector's Address [*Rektoratsrede*]" of 1933. And it is also here that Heidegger returns to a full-fledged embrace of the term *Geist*, which Heidegger claims can only be said and understood in German because only the German language associates spirit with flame (HQ 45). After the period of the rectorship and Heidegger's open association with Nazism comes a long period (which has recently been examined in depth in a whole range of studies) when Heidegger abjures once again any usage of the word *Geist*. Derrida's analysis tracks the different forms (*geistig*, *geistlich*, and so on) by which the word asserts its "ghostly" presence in various of Heidegger's works, until the essay on the poetry of Georg Trakl (1953), when Heidegger once again returns to the language of spirit and flame. Heidegger, in this essay, says for example: "Inasmuch as the nature of spirit consists in a bursting into flame, it strikes a new course, lights it, and sets man on the way" ("Language in the Poem" 179–80). The effect of reading such statements in the context of Derrida's patient explication of the whole range of Heidegger's work, which is not without its attentiveness to historical circumstance, is very powerful. It might be one thing to speak of the specifically German spirit as flame in 1933, but to use such language in 1953 raises the question of whether Heidegger learned anything at all from his involvement in the history of his time. Derrida's own discourse, however, does not rest with identifying and demonizing Heidegger's Nazi past. Rather, he sees the attraction of such a philosophical discourse opening up as an abyss for thinking: "We have here a program and a combinatory whose power remains abyssal. In all rigor, it exculpates none of the discourses which can thus exchange their power. It leaves no place open for any arbitrating authority. Nazism was not born in the desert. We all know this, but it has to be constantly recalled" (HQ 138–39; trans. 109). Now, one could always turn aside from such a statement and say that Derrida is presenting a "defense" of Heidegger (see Norris WWP 242). The "impossible" ethics of deconstruction, however, demands that one continue to think about the issues involved in their full, abysslike complexity, a complexity that denies any firm ground upon which to maintain one's own lack of involvement in the very issues raised by the inquiry.

Although Derrida rarely, if ever, invokes the Holocaust, he has begun to speak, if cryptically, of what remains after a holocaust. Cinders are what remain, but they retain the unassimilable memory of fire. Fire stands in a relationship of *exteriority* to cinders. Cinders may be "warm" or "cold" but in any event no longer retain any "identity," much like the structure of the sign. Or, as Derrida puts this, "The name 'cinder' is still a cinder of the cinder itself" (*Cinders* 49). Even the *feu* of *Feu la cendre* is implicated in this relationship between flame and ashes. Although in the grammatical combination of the title, *feu* is more likely to call up the outdated, literary meaning of "formerly," the association with ash means that flame resides there as a kind of ghostly background.[17] Or, as Derrida says, "No cinder without fire [Pas de cendre sans feu]" (*Cinders* 37). One consequence of Derrida's examination of Heidegger's writings on spirit, perhaps not the least, is that ashes will *always* bear this association with flame. There is no writing by Derrida on *cendre* that is not also a meditation on the Holocaust.

Why should the Greek name of *holocaust* have been given to the collective experience of twentieth-century European Jews? Just what is a holocaust? How is it to be thought? The longest single self-citation in Derrida's *Feu la cendre* (*Cinders*) is from *Glas* (*Glas* 265–70; *Cinders* 42–48). In this meditation, Derrida moves from Hegel's writings on the history of religion, to a questioning of the "all-burning" sacrifice (*brûle-tout, holocauste, Opfer*), to an association of the holocaust with the thinking of the gift (*es gibt*) in Heidegger. Should there have been any doubt that Derrida in *Glas* was trying to think the most difficult ethical questions, the repetition of this passage (not a simple repetition, of course, but a taking up, an iteration, a citation) in the context of *Cinders* should help to alleviate it. Or not. Perhaps that doubt *is* the ethical question, the question of what ethics is, the *question* of ethics.[18]

Afterword

The discussion in these last two chapters, beginning with the questions, *What is intersubjective violence?* and, *Is Derrida pointing to a kind of ethics that in practice would be unattainable?* eventually leads to a complex understanding in which these two questions can be seen as different versions of the same problem. Any inquiry, even the most patient, attentive, respectful deconstructive reading, is inevitably violent, even though such a deconstruction aims at what I have called *a self-articulating resistance to intersubjective violence.* Intersubjective violence is not an abstraction—as Derrida's increasing turn towards an autobiographical siting of his discourse may be seen to insist upon—but a way of identifying real-world situations in which actual people suffer real harm. Such violence as occurs in textual form may be gentler than other effects of "writing" that Derrida shows at work in the political, economic, religious, and domestic spheres. To say that these forms of "writing" are always already at work, in advance of and in a strong sense determining what we can do, say, or write, is a version of the Foucauldian analysis of power/knowledge relations operative within discursive networks. The ethical practice that the late Foucault urged take place in practices of the self would be another way to describe a self-articulating resistance to intersubjective violence. The problem with which Derrida and Foucault both are dealing is the impossibility of saying in advance what those practices should be. The impossibility of ethics does not mean that ethical behavior *per se* is impossible or undesirable, but rather that normative ethical systems based on prescriptive descriptions or phrases are caught within discursive networks of "power/knowledge" (Foucault) or "writing" (Derrida) that in turn are based on necessarily violent—though usually not acknowledged as such—substructures and histories.[19]

The question of "How to avoid speaking?" (see *Psyché* 535–95) addresses the Levinasian paradox that only in discourse is one's subjectivity engaged, yet one must always be open first to "the call of the other." The ethical response to this dilemma is "impossible" and yet is always being articulated—in ways that exceed the limits of the individual, rational, willing subject, and that language opens the way for, but never guarantees.[20] *The ethical subject of discourse* is the subject that articulates (demonstrates and expresses) this dilemma in response to the highest ethical demand. In this way postmodern theory moves past the impasses of the enlightenment view of "man" in the direction of a subject that "first" responds to *alterity*, an other that is truly other. The "impossible" ethics of deconstruction points to the closure of the system of "writing" that Derrida announced in the *Grammatology*. That there is nothing outside of this system means *not* that everything really takes place in books, but that every human response (even the writing of books) is always an ethical response, caught up in conflicting networks of power, violence, and domination. The ethical subject is always already caught and defined by such frameworks that are not of one's conscious choice or making, but that nonetheless demand more choice and decision-making than one could ever possibly accomplish, and that one must attempt to undertake as one's ethical responsibility.

Notes

Introduction

1. I present a version of this by-now common argument in the introduction to *Obdurate Brilliance* (2–7). See also Paul Smith's *Discerning the Subject* for a version somewhat different from my own.

2. Citing Nietzsche's *The Wanderer and His Shadow*, Foucault demonstrates his understanding of the Nietzschean critique: "Further, genealogical analysis shows that the concept of liberty is an 'invention of the ruling classes' and not fundamental to man's nature or at the root of his attachment to being and truth. What is found at the historical beginning of things is not the inviolable identity of their origin; it is the dissension of other things. It is disparity" (NGH 142).

3. Habermas's tone is not as positive, or even neutral, as I have tried to be in summarizing his position. He says, for example: "Nietzsche's critique of modernity has been continued along both paths. The sceptical scholar who wants to unmask the perversion of the will to power, the revolt of reactionary forces, and the emergence of a subject-centered reason by using anthropological, psychological, and historical methods has successors in Bataille, Lacan, and Foucault; the initiate-critic of metaphysics who pretends to a unique kind of knowledge and pursues the rise of the philosophy of the subject back to its pre-Socratic origins has successors in Heidegger and Derrida" (PDM 97).

4. Foucault, for example, says: "The search for a form of morality that would be acceptable to everyone—in the sense that everyone would have to submit to it—strikes me as catastrophic" (*Foucault Live* 330).

5. As Derrida comments, "The phrase which for some reason has become a sort of slogan, in general, so badly understood, of deconstruction ('there is nothing outside the text'), means nothing else: there is nothing outside context" (*Limited Inc.* 136).

6. I address the Kristevan model of text production in *Modern Poetic Practice* (14–15).

7. Luce Irigaray gives a more precise analysis of this question by introducing

the term *sexuation* as a means of identifying the gendered aspects of theoretical writings, especially Freud (see particularly *Ce sexe* 71; *Éthique de la différence sexuelle* 127–28.)

8. I am thinking here particularly of the volume edited by Diana Fuss, *Inside/ Out: Lesbian Theories, Gay Theories.*

9. Many of these questions are raised, for example, in the texts by Geoffrey Bennington and Derrida published in *Jacques Derrida*, especially Derrida's contribution, "Circonfession."

10. For a French version of the thinking of Derrida, Foucault, and others as a historically contingent aberration, see Luc Ferry and Alain Renaut, *La pensée 68.*

11. These are not only critics on the right. William V. Spanos, for example, argues that "Heideggerian *destruction,* whatever Heidegger's specific sociopolitical application, is *inherently more adequate* than deconstruction to the radical emancipatory task of contemporary oppositional intellectuals" (82) and concludes that "in textualizing the ontological difference—in reducing the difference that temporality disseminates all across the indissoluble continuum of being to *différance*—deconstruction 'after' Derrida has precluded itself from becoming a historically material transdisciplinary *praxis*" (102, my italics).

Chapter One

1. Here is Henry Staten, quoting and interpreting Wittgenstein on this issue: "Whenever I point to an object and say a word, the act is meaningless except insofar as 'the place is already prepared' (PI §31) for this word; that is, insofar as there exists a language within which such specific games as naming or saying 'This!' make sense" (69).

2. "La culture occidentale a constitué, sous le nom d'homme, un être qui, par un seul et même jeu de raisons, doit être domaine positif du *savoir* et ne peut pas être objet de *science*" (378; my translation).

3. Preceding this, Wittgenstein says: "What should strike us about this expression is the phrase 'always I.' Always *who?*—For, queer enough, I don't mean: 'always L. W.' This leads us to considering the criteria for the identity of a person" (*The Blue and Brown Books* 61).

4. Derrida, in an interview, states: "I totally refuse the label of nihilism which has been ascribed to me and my American colleagues. Deconstruction is not an enclosure in nothingness, but an openness towards the other" ("Deconstruction and the Other" 124).

5. Harry E. Stewart, for example, in part through the use of published court records, questions the veracity of Genet's claims to have written his first two novels while in prison. Edmund White's recent biography, *Genet,* also has recourse to the official documentation, but White manages to maintain a much more nuanced view of the interactions between the Genet who appears in official records and the one who appears as a self-invention in his texts.

6. In a recent interview, Derrida insists on this widespread view of deconstruction as a motivated misreading: "I would say that the idea that deconstruction should confine itself to the analysis of the discursive text—I know that the idea is widespread—is really either a gross misunderstanding or a political strategy designed to limit deconstruction to matters of language. Deconstruction starts with the deconstruction of logocentrism, and thus to want to confine it to linguistic phenomena is the most suspect of operations" ("The Spatial Arts," DVA 15).

7. Charles E. Scott analyzes the implication of the knowing subject in the network of power relations and suffering that goes under the name of *aesthesis* (117).

8. Derrida comments on the violence of his response to Searle, "And if, as I believe, violence remains in fact (almost) ineradicable, its analysis and the most refined, ingenious account of its conditions will be the least violent gestures, perhaps even nonviolent, and in any case those which contribute most to transforming the legal-ethical-political rules: *in* the university and *outside* the university" ("Afterword," *Limited Inc.* 112).

9. The crucial formulation of this critique is made by Edward Said (219–22; cf. Paul Bové 141ff.).

10. "Le fait nu que . . . l'homme, isolé ou en groupe, soit devenu objet de science,—cela ne peut pas être considéré ni traité comme un phénomène d'opinion: c'est un événement dans l'ordre du savoir" (356; my translation).

11. "Si la découverte du Retour est bien la fin de la philosophie, *la fin de l'homme,* elle, est le retour du commencement de la philosophie. De nos jours on ne peut plus penser que dans le vide de l'homme disparu. Car ce vide ne creuse pas un manque; il ne prescrit pas une lacune à combler. Il n'est rien de plus, rien de moins, que le dépli d'un espace où il est enfin à nouveau possible de penser" (353; my translation; my italics).

12. Deleuze explains, with his customary elegance of expression: "It is a question of general method: instead of moving from an apparent exteriority to a 'kernel of interiority' which would be essential, one must conjure up the illusory interiority in order to restore words and things to their constitutive exteriority" (*Foucault* 50; my translation).

13. "Entre techniques de savoir et stratégies de pouvoir, nulle extériorité, même si elles ont leur rôle spécifique et qu'elles s'articulent l'une sur l'autre, *à partir de leur différence*" (VS 130; my translation).

14. In the illuminating "Afterword: The Subject and Power," Foucault states that "In itself, the use of power is not violence" (Dreyfus and Rabinow 220).

15. In "The Ethic of Care for the Self" Foucault specifically addresses Habermas's model of communicative rationality: "The thought that there could be a state of communication which would be such that the games of truth could circulate freely, without obstacles, without constraint and without coercive effects, seems to me to be Utopia" (129).

16. For an overview of the range of feminist responses to Foucault, see the volume edited by Diamond and Quinby, *Feminism and Foucault*.

17. See, for example, Fuss's quick and pointed analysis of Scholes's "critical chivalry" in his opposition of deconstruction to feminism (Fuss 26).

18. Not an assessment with which Derrida would agree. See, in particular, his stinging attack on Habermas, among others, in the long footnote to "Like the Sound of the Sea Deep within a Shell: Paul de Man's War." Derrida says, for example, "It is *always* in the name of ethics—a supposedly democratic ethics of discussion—it is always in the name of transparent communication and 'consensus' that the most brutal disregard of the elementary rules of discussion is produced. . . . The most visible example of this is . . . Habermas" (259n).

19. My own view is that this question is largely a nonissue, though I discuss some of the arguments surrounding it more fully in chapter 6.

20. For Derrida's discussion of the Kantian principle of analogy as a bridge (Brücke), see *La vérité en peinture* (43). A more meditative discussion of bridges, specifically those on the Cornell University campus, can be found in his "Principle of Reason." Irene Harvey briefly discusses this link between Kant's thinking and Derrida's (17).

21. "Étant donné cette structure d'itération, l'intention qui anime l'énonciation ne sera jamais de part en part présente à elle-même et à son contenu. L'itération qui la structure a priori y introduit une déhiscence et une brisure essentielles. Le 'non-sérieux,' l'*oratio obliqua* ne pourront plus être exclus, comme le souhaitait Austin, du langage 'ordinaire'" (M 389).

22. Norris's discussion of Fish is a response to Fish's *Doing What Comes Naturally: Change, Rhetoric and the Practice of Theory in Literary and Legal Studies* (1989).

23. The hermeneutic circle as a horizon of understanding is a persistent construct throughout Derrida's work and one of the key ways that, as Derrida has repeatedly stated, much of his work operates in the line or "way" of thinking opened up by Heidegger. See, for example, Derrida's remarks following his delivery of his "Différance" lecture to the *Société Française de Philosophie* (trans. in Wood and Bernasconi, 83–95; esp. 86).

24. This understanding of the distinction between complete stasis and the possibility of evolution in Fish's theory is expressed with admirable clarity by Drucilla Cornell. She says: "The result of Fish's position is that social criticism and radical transformation are impossible. For Fish, to have social criticism in legal interpretation or a critical observer, let alone a standpoint by which to know when 'real' transformation had happened, we would have to appeal to a transcendental viewpoint. Since we have no *transcendental* or *outside* viewpoint, it follows that there can be no social criticism and no critical consciousness. Change can take place only as slow evolution, but not through transformation, and the players may well never note the change. The system is run

differently, but there is no true *difference* from the system. There is only evolution, not transformation" (PL 145). Norris makes the reductive leap from the evolutionary model that Cornell here ascribes (correctly, I think) to Fish and a static model.

25. I dispute this general characterization of hermeneutics, in the context of the interpretation of contemporary poetry, in "'To disarm the cryptogram'."

26. Norris's proof that de Man's theories can be used to support social-praxis theory is strangely deferred in Norris's own writings. See, in addition, *Paul de Man* (16) and *The Contest of the Faculties* (40–46; 185–88). Norris's large claim concerning de Man's link to the social-praxis theory is treated in roughly the same terms in all three of these texts, that is, as though it had already been thoroughly demonstrated elsewhere. It would be my contention that in none of these texts does Norris even *attempt* to prove his claim with anything like the rigor he implies.

27. In *Paul de Man* (1988), published two years prior to WWP, Norris actually demonstrates a keen understanding of Derrida's text (see especially *Paul de Man* 193–98).

28. I refer, of course, to the discovery and subsequent publication of de Man's *Wartime Journalism* (a text I reviewed in the *American Book Review*), and all of the ensuing aftermath. Geoffrey Galt Harpham has offered a compelling interpretation of Derrida's response to de Man's wartime writings that extends what I offer here as tentative reservations (see "Derrida and the Ethics of Criticism," esp. 396–97).

Chapter Two

1. I maintain this spelling of *chiasma* as opposed to *chiasmus* or *chiasm* (cf. Hadreas and Schmidt) because it usefully distinguishes the properly philosophical notion (*chiasma*) from the rhetorical device (*chiasmus*). *Chiasm* seems to be an acceptable alternate spelling for the latter, but not for the former, according to Webster's and the OED.

2. Jean-François Lyotard, in *La condition postmoderne* and "Histoire universelle et différences culturelles," argues that philosophy can no longer be the organizing metanarrative, or "récit des récits."

3. A full discussion of Merleau-Ponty's relation to individual figures in the philosophical tradition is out of the range of my discussion. See Hadreas, Sichère, and Descombes for this issue.

4. The source of the actual statement is possibly ambiguous. Here is the full statement: "Et comme la genèse du corps objectif n'est qu'un moment dans la constitution de l'objet, le corps, en se retirant du monde objectif, entraînera les fils intentionnels qui le relient à son entourage et finalement nous révélera *le sujet percevant comme le monde perçu*" (PP 86; my italics). The final italicized phrase is what I translate as *the body is the perceived world*.

5. The translators, inexplicably, leave out this last phrase of Descombes.

6. Descombes shows his idealizing bias even more clearly in the following series of steps: "Merleau-Ponty insists on the return to a 'true *cogito,*' namely the 'I perceive' beneath the 'I think.' The origin of truth is particular, relative, *human.* But then the phenomenon is only a semblance, or the opinion that I, *myself,* . . . can hold about things" (MA 86; MFP 68).

7. I take Merleau-Ponty's "later philosophy" to mean primarily two works, "Eye and Mind" (EM), [*L'Oeil et l'Esprit* (OE)], and *The Visible and the Invisible* (VI trans.) [*Le Visible et l'invisible* (VI)], already cited.

8. See Charles Bernstein's very interesting paraphrase of this passage in his "Artifice of Absorption" (87). Bernstein is interested in testing this model of "obscurity," or what he sometimes calls "impermeability," in the context of the reception of experimental writing.

9. The most poignant example is the strange lapse in Bernard Sichère's rigorous (and even reverent) study, *Merleau-Ponty: Ou le corps de la philosophie,* where he uses what might be termed a "vulgar Lacanian" approach to psychoanalyze Merleau-Ponty's philosophy of *flesh* as a "symptom" of infantile regression, based on a "fantasm" of primal unity (209–14).

10. Derrida offers an extended critique of Merleau-Ponty's theory of signs in his earliest published work, *Edmund Husserl's Origin of Geometry: An Introduction* (trans. 111ff.). My view is that Merleau-Ponty represents for Derrida a certain version of phenomenology, one with which he has an extremely conflicted relationship, and that this in turn accounts for the almost complete absence of reference to Merleau-Ponty after a certain stage of his work.

11. For the accuracy to Lacan's thought of using "it" as the pronoun for the subject, see Gary Handwerk, "The Irony of Double Vision: Lacan's Liquidation of the Subject."

12. Slavoj Žižek bases much of his tantalizing Lacanian discourse on this premise.

13. James Schmidt, for example, states: "Merleau-Ponty still clung to the pre-Freudian tendency to equate 'consciousness' . . . with 'subjectivity' and thus to ignore the important role played by the unconscious processes in the creation of the subject" (76–77).

14. For example: "Car il ne suffit pas d'en décider par son effet: la Mort. Il s'agit encore de savoir quelle mort, celle que porte la vie ou celle qui la porte [Because it is not enough to judge by its effect: Death. It's still a matter of knowing which death, that which life carries, or that which carries it]" (E 810; my translation). I have discussed the content of this statement (Baker, *Modern Poetic Practice,* 38–39). Jane Gallop remarks on Lacan's use of chiasmus, especially the phrase, "The meaning of a return to Freud is the return to the meaning of Freud" (Gallop 93–94). Derrida is no stranger to the chiasmus, either. See his statement, "χ(le chiasme) (qu'on pourra toujours considérer,

hâtivement, comme le dessein thématique de la dissémination. . . .) [(χ (The chiasmus) (which can be considered a quick thematic diagram of dissemination)]" (*La dissémination* 52; trans. 44).

15. We might compare this to Wittgenstein's remark: "'True' and 'false' in a dream. I dream that it is raining, and that I say 'it is raining'—on the other hand: I dream that I say 'I am dreaming'" (*Zettel* §398).

16. Lacan states: "Read, for example, the note concerning what he calls the turning inside-out of the finger of a glove [see Merleau-Ponty, VI 316–18; trans. 263–64], in as much as it seems to appear there—note the way in which the leather envelops the fur in a winter glove—that consciousness, in its illusion of *seeing itself seeing itself*, finds its basis in the inside-out structure of the gaze" (XI 78; FF 82).

Chapter Three

1. As Mark Taylor says: "By attempting to think difference as same, Heidegger seems to extend the philosophical search for origins. In exploring the difference left unthought by philosophy, Heidegger seeks what he explicitly labels an 'essential origin.' From this point of view, the problem with the traditional notion of Being, as well as its modern manifestation in phenomenology's 'principle of principles' (i.e. transcendental subjectivity), is that both Being and subjectivity are *insufficiently* primordial, and, hence, cannot provide a proper foundation for thinking. As a more original origin, difference can answer the question of how presence becomes present" ("Introduction" DC 21).

2. For a more extended discussion by Taylor, see especially "Cleaving: Martin Heidegger" (A 35–58).

3. In a very similar way, Derrida will call for a reading of previous philosophers that conserves and preserves their "legibility": "Pour penser radicalement le jeu, il faut donc d'abord *épuiser* sérieusement la problématique ontologique et transcendentale . . . suivre effectivement et jusqu'au bout le mouvement des questions husserlienne et heideggerienne, leur conserver leur efficace et leur lisibilité [To think play radically the ontological and transcendental problematics must first be seriously *exhausted* . . . the critical movement of the Husserlian and Heideggerian questions must be effectively followed to the very end, and their effectiveness and legibility must be conserved]" (G 73; trans. 50). This statement would also serve to refute Christopher Norris's attempt to dissociate Derrida from Heidegger's thinking that I discuss in chapter 1.

4. Derrida alludes briefly to Hegel's use of this verbal form, and Koyré's commentary on it in the latter's French translation of Hegel's *Logic*. Hegel's phrase with Koyré's translation reads: "mais c'est là un rapport absolumment différent du simple (sondern es ist absolut differente Beziehung) [but in this is a relationship absolutely different from the simple]" ("La différance" M 14–15; trans. 14). So it may be that the famous unheard "a" of "différance" stems from

Derrida's conversation with Hegel and Heidegger. For Hegel as a philosopher of difference, see Mark C. Taylor (esp. E 98).

5. Descombes uses the "post-Kantian" label in order to insist that the introduction of the category of time is a Kantian move. He says, for example, "This decidedly post-Kantian 'philosophy of difference' is essentially a 'doctrine of the faculties' (read, faculties *of the subject*]" (MA 185–86n; MFP 158n).

6. Descombes claims that Derridean "difference" is finally indistinguishable from Hegelian Identity of this type: "Now the identity of difference and non-difference is indistinguishable from the identity (posited by Hegel) of identity and non-identity" (MA 178; MFP 152). This statement shows that Descombes remains firmly within the closure of the concept and that his analytical approach is inadequate for a full understanding of Derrida.

7. Deleuze states: "Difference is not diversity. Diversity is given. But difference is that by which what is given is given. That by which what is given is given as diverse. Difference is not the phenomenon, but the closest noumenon to the phenomenon" (DR 286). This is part of a brilliant disquisition given the Kantian premises, but one senses a certain strain in the language.

8. See Descombes's comment on Deleuze's use of the phrase the "*concept* of difference" (MA 182n; MFP 155–56n).

9. He will say elsewhere: "As for the concept of experience, it is most unwieldy here. Like all the notions I am using here, it belongs to the history of metaphysics and we can only use it under erasure [sous rature]" (G 89; trans. 60). I might note that many of Derrida's analyses of earlier philosophers seem to be strategically apt ways of confronting his near-contemporaries such as Sartre or Merleau-Ponty without directly referring to their works.

10. As Heidegger says, "For language is the most delicate and thus the most susceptible vibration holding everything within the suspended structure of the appropriation. We dwell in the appropriation inasmuch as our active nature is given over to language [Insofern unser Wesen in die Sprache vereignet ist, wohnen wir im Ereignis]" (ID 38, 102).

11. The Husserlian heritage of speech and the voice is clearly represented in the late writings of Maurice Merleau-Ponty, as when he writes of becoming "a sonorous being [un être sonore]" (VI 190; trans. 144). I have suggested some of the limitations of Merleau-Ponty's theory of language and expression in chapter 2.

12. The difference between the Kantian *a priori* and the Derridean notion of the *trace* should not be overlooked, nor made into an identity. Christopher Norris states, for example, "Derrida's version of this Kantian argument makes writing . . . the precondition of all possible knowledge" (*Derrida* 95). I would argue that Derrida's *writing*, or the inscription of the subject within a whole range of economic, religious, and political systems, *precedes* the constitution of the individual subject and so is radically non-Kantian. Writing is an exteriority

made interior; the Kantian *a priori* are universal categories of the interior made exterior.

13. The first italicized phrase, "un passé qui n'a jamais été présent [a past which has never been present]", Derrida attributes to Emmanuel Levinas, but it was certainly first used by Merleau-Ponty (PP 71; see Taylor DC 25).

14. Norris's study, *Derrida*, is admirable for the way it focuses attention on what he claims is the neglected ethical dimension of Derrida's work. Norris also maintains—mistakenly, I think—that we must remain within a rather fixed sphere of "reason" and thus be able to establish determinate meanings in order to realize the full value of such an ethical dimension. The Derridean challenge to thought and action, I would claim, is rather how to maintain an ethical stance precisely by acknowledging and making use of the play of presence and absence opened up by *différance*.

15. See also, Leavy et al., *Glossary*. Following the practice established in the latter, citations refer to the left (Hegel) and right (Genet) sides as *a* and *b*, respectively. All page numbers refer to the first French edition, followed by the reference for the translation, which I have modified in places.

Chapter Four

1. For a discussion of the religious aspect of Levinas's thought in the context of critical theory, see Jacques Derrida, "Violence et métaphysique (essai sur la pensée d'Emmanuel Levinas)" in *L'Écriture et la différence* [ED] (*Writing and Difference* [WD]). Levinas's religious thought is intricately related to that of Martin Buber, especially *I and Thou*.

2. These issues are related to the model of *exteriority* that I use interpretively when analyzing modernist and postmodern long poems in *Obdurate Brilliance*.

3. See, for example, Lacan's discussion of the *"ne explétif"* in relation to Oedipus (VII 353ff.). See also Jacques Lacan, "La chose freudienne" (*Écrits* 401–36).

4. For a more extended discussion of Lacan on desire, see my "Desire and the Forms of Poetic Expression" (*Modern Poetic Practice* 67–76).

5. As Mark Taylor states, commenting on Levinas: "The face that the I/eye encounters is always the face of an other" (A 210).

6. Robert Bernasconi presents a different view of this essay, claiming that it exhibits self-deconstructive strategies, "but Derrida's essay can also be read so that it ceases to have the appearance of either an internal critique or a critique from a standpoint situated outside the essay and instead already exhibits the double strategy of deconstruction" ("The Trace of Levinas in Derrida" 16). See also Bernasconi's examination of ethical issues in early and later Derrida ("No More Stories" 162).

7. For a depth analysis of this topography in Lacan's theory of the *moi*, see

Jacqueline Rose, "The Imaginary" (in *Sexuality in the Field of Vision*, esp. 184–90).

8. I examine the sexuation of poetic language as an example of nonoppositional difference in chapter 3 of *Obdurate Brilliance*.

9. References to *The Différend* are to numbered paragraphs [§], except where page numbers are indicated [pp.].

10. For the question of *métarécits* and the legitimation of knowledge in Lyotard's thinking, see *La Condition postmoderne* [CP].

11. As Lyotard says, "Consensus has become a outmoded and suspect value. But justice as a value is neither outmoded nor suspect. We must thus arrive at an idea and practice of justice that is not linked to those of consensus [Le consensus est devenu une valeur désuète, et suspecte. Ce qui ne l'est pas, c'est la justice. Il faut donc parvenir à une idée et à une pratique de la justice qui ne soit pas liée à celles du consensus]" (CP 106; trans. 66 modified).

12. Lyotard, of course, began as a phenomenologist; see, for example, his early work, *La phénoménologie*.

13. Levinas says, "Through sexuality the subject enters into relation with what is absolutely other" (TI 254; trans. 276 modified). This leads to Derrida's speculation that *Totality and Infinity* could only have been written by a man (ED 228n; WD 320–21n92).

14. Irigaray's direct discussion of Levinas (EDS 173–99) is not so much an analysis as a lyrical riff on themes by Levinas.

15. In a reference to Heidegger's idea that each era has one primary issue, Irigaray terms sexual difference "one of the questions if not the question for thinking in our era" (EDS 13).

16. Alice Jardine has theorized in *Gynesis* that the entire movement of critical discourse by men in what she calls "modernity" is enabled by a paradigm based on sexual difference.

Chapter Five

1. Kelly Oliver provides a useful overview of this complex debate within Anglo-American feminism in her Introduction to *Reading Kristeva* (1–17).

2. Kelly Oliver presents a version of Kristeva's ethical theories, with important implications for feminist practice, as what Oliver terms "outlaw ethics" (181–89). Drucilla Cornell presents a compelling version of ethical feminism, as when she says: "Ethical feminism denies the 'truth' of the gender hierarchy by affirming the feminine within sexual difference as other to its current identifications" (*Transformations* 142).

3. Claudia Card, in her introductory essay to a volume on feminist ethics, uses a different term to describe what I am here calling "normative" feminism, as when she says: "Conservative gynocentrism has not found a voice in this volume" (17).

4. Nancy Chodorow and Susan Contralto give this position, which Gilbert and Gubar share with other "normative" feminists, a pointed critique: "It is as if notions that the personal is the political have been interpreted to mean that almost primal fantasies constitute feminist politics or theory" (Chodorow 80).

5. The differences between Kristeva's theory of abjection and the sanitized version of the same stage offered by "object-relations" theory are illustrated in this statement by Nancy Chodorow: "On the physical level, the infant comes to be unproblematically aware of its own boundaries and separateness" (157). Significantly, Chodorow does not mention or cite Kristeva in her collection, *Feminism and Psychoanalytic Theory*, not even in her very brief discussion of "Lacanian feminism" (187–89).

6. But Kristeva had pointed to this positioning of women vis-à-vis the symbolic order at least as early as her statements in "Women's Time," such as: "In sum, all of these considerations—her eternal debt to the woman-mother—make a woman more vulnerable within the symbolic order, more fragile when she suffers within it, more virulent when she protects herself from it" (204–205).

7. As to the questions, Why literature? and, Why women in relation to literature?—see Kristeva (WT 207). I will return to the unconscious, dream aspect of this identificatory structure later in my analysis of *The Silence of the Lambs*.

8. As Leslie Hill succinctly puts it: "Kristeva analyses the case of Céline as representing a risk inherent in all avant-garde literary practice, should the negativity of rejection turn into abjection and give rise to a paranoid delirium rather than ethically responsible fictional production" (154).

9. As Kristeva says: "Finally, there is also the connivance of the young girl with her mother, her greater difficulty than the boy in detaching herself from the mother in order to accede to the order of signs as invested by the absence and separation constitutive of the paternal function" (WT 204).

10. In discussing Kristeva's use of the terms *metaphor* and *metonymy* to characterize love and desire, respectively, in *Histoires d'amour*, Barzilai says: "In contrast to Lacan, who emphasizes the metonymic dimension of desire, the displacements imposed by a third party, the mythic father of *Totem and Taboo*, Kristeva investigates—through her condensed interpretations—the metaphoric dimension of love: the bond with (as well as separation from) the mother" (302).

11. Kristeva's more recent analytically oriented writings maintain this stance on ethics: "But in practicing an ethics which has nothing to do with that of punitive legislation, the analyst recognizes the reality of the depressive position and, by affirming the symbolic legitimacy of her pain, permits the patient to seek other means, symbolic or imaginary, to elaborate her suffering" (*Soleil noir* 97; my translation).

12. More than fifteen years after the landmark publication of *Révolution du*

langage poétique, we are now just beginning to catch up with the full scope of a remarkable, ongoing career. See especially John Lechte ("Art, Love and Melancholy"), Noreen O'Connor, Alison Ainley, and Leslie Hill.

13. Geoffrey Galt Harpham has proposed a version of this linguistic argument, with which I am generally more sympathetic. He says, for instance, "We are ethical subjects living in ethical worlds because we are linguistic subjects" ("Language, History and Ethics" 146). Miller's own recent article, "Derrida's Topographies," likewise presents a version of deconstructive ethics with which I have more sympathy.

14. Albert Cook has written a searching critique of Booth, in the wide context of this and other issues relating to the ethical dimension of literature (see esp. 134–35).

15. A more recent essay by Altieri, "Frank Stella and Jacques Derrida," moves away from the personhood argument and more toward a deconstructive ethics.

16. In *Sexual/Textual Politics,* Toril Moi puts Kristeva forth as the leading feminist thinker at the intersection of psychoanalysis, feminism, and literary practice. Yet Moi does criticize Kristeva's project for its lack of *political* direction: "In a political context her emphasis on the semiotic as an unconscious force precludes any analysis of the conscious decision-making processes that must be part of any *collective* revolutionary project" (170). Kristeva distrusts the *thetic* positioning implied by Moi's "conscious decision-making processes," no less than she distrusts the "normative" ethics necessary to a "*collective* revolutionary project." In describing the work of Marguerite Duras, Kristeva says: "Politics is not . . . the field in which human freedom is deployed. . . . The modern political domain is massively, totalitarianly social, leveling, killing" (*Soleil noir,* 242; my translation).

17. The construction of the viewer's subjectivity is of course a massive topic. See Jacqueline Rose and Teresa de Lauretis. The classic essay on the "male gaze" by Laura Mulvey forms the point of departure for the essays in a recent collection edited by Patricia Erens.

18. Whether Kristeva, in fact, privileges a heterosexual subject position is unclear to me. Clearly, Judith Butler believes she does, and this disagreement forms the foundation for her stinging indictment of Kristeva's overall theory (Butler, GT 79–93).

19. *The Silence of the Lambs* presents a complexly constructed viewer position, in notable contrast to another film released around the same time, *Thelma and Louise* (directed by Ridley Scott; 1991), which clearly maintains the "male gaze" while utilizing female protagonists. The ensuing controversy over the film, and especially whether these characters should be seen as role models, shows to my mind the logical and pragmatic limitations of what we might call role-model feminism (see Maslin).

20. Diana Fuss's recent work on the essentialist/constructionist binarism

underlying feminist theories maintains a keen awareness of the dangers of prescribing normative goals and behaviors (29).

Chapter Six

1. Simon Critchley nicely describes this traditional approach: "When one thinks of ethics in its traditional determination, one imagines a collection of laws, principles, and moral rules which habitually have some claim to universality and are thus meant to prescribe human action" ("The Chiasmus," 102). Derrida explains some of his reasons for avoiding the term "ethics" in an exchange in the collective volume, *Altérités*, but then goes on to link his thinking on these issues to Levinas's "non-traditional" use of the term (see esp. *Altérités* 70–71).

2. Derrida has offered a significant statement on this problematic in the context of legal studies in "Force of Law." In the shortest possible (and therefore circular) form, the argument of this essay, as I read it, is that constituted legal authority can never serve as a completely satisfactory (or *just*) recourse for societal violence because violence arises in the same process by which authority is constituted. This leads to the need for thinking justice as always necessarily *aporetic*, or always "to-come [à-venir]" ("Force of Law" 27). Derrida's thinking on justice thus parallels some of his recent statements on democracy, such as when he invokes "a democracy that must have the structure of a promise—*and thus the memory of that which carries the future, the to-come, here and now* [une démocratie qui doit avoir la structure de la promise—*et donc la mémoire de ce qui porte l'avenir ici maintenant*]" (*L'autre cap* 76; trans. 78; italics in the original).

3. Mark Taylor's review essay on Gasché's text begins, "*The Tain of the Mirror* is a *serious* book" ("Foiling Reflections," in *Tears* 87–103).

4. Derrida seems to have anticipated this exclusion (in an interview from 1976); the reason he gives there for staging the encounter between Hegel and Genet in *Glas* has to do with introducing what is "*irrecevable*" into the text of philosophy: both to thematize and to exemplify what the philosophical discourse is prepared (or not) to allow in (see *Points de suspension* 24–25). Derrida's other significant essays on Hegel include "Le puits et la pyramide" (M 79–127; trans. 69–108), and "De l'économie restreinte à l'économie générale: Un hegelianisme sans réserve" (ED 369–407; WD 251–77).

5. Hillis Miller has offered a definitive refutation, it seems to me, of this view in his recent essay, "Derrida's Topographies."

6. I make reference to Derrida's discussion of Genet in my "Metric, Naming and Exile: Perse / Pound / Genet."

7. Another way to say this is that Gasché's discussion of heterology in Plato and Derrida won't even begin to help us to comprehend what happened, for example, in the case of the Los Angeles police officers charged with beating

Rodney King and the subsequent riots in Los Angeles. One recalls Genet's meeting with the Black Panthers in the early seventies that he describes at some length in *Un captif amoureux* (see also Edmund White, *Genet*, 521–40).

8. I thus agree with Rorty that Gasché relies too much on the propositional weight of single words, instead of the sentences in which those words develop relational meaning (see Rorty, "Is Derrida a Transcendental Philosopher?" 124). Another way to say this is Kierkegaard's statement in *Fear and Trembling*: "I for my part have applied considerable time to understanding Hegelian philosophy and believe that I have understood it fairly well; I am sufficiently brash to think that when I cannot understand particular passages despite all my pains, he himself may not have been entirely clear" (33).

9. The article by Sharon Marcus, which I discuss beginning with the next paragraph, contains references to the scholarship on rape and "rape culture."

10. The first and perhaps still the most notable example of this tendency is Geoffrey Hartman's *Saving the Text*.

11. I believe that the blurring of the boundary distinction between philosophy and literature, at least in the way the problem is defined by Habermas, is a philosophical nonissue. Rorty says something like this when he questions how one even goes about defining philosophy. In his view, one either draws up a list of names that represent the philosphical tradition, or one looks at all the different kinds of activities that go under the name of philosophy. He continues, "Only if one buys in on the logocentric idea that there just *must* be an autonomous discipline which adjudicates ultimate questions would 'philosophy' have a third sense, one appropriate for Gasché's purposes. It is only by reference to some such idea that it makes sense to worry, as he does, about the lines between philosophy and literature" ("Is Derrida a Transcendental Philosopher?" 122). I discuss some of Derrida's statements on this issue later in the chapter.

12. Derrida establishes his distance from the French phenomenological tradition, of which Merleau-Ponty at the time was a leading representative, in his first published work, his translation and introduction to Husserl's *Origin of Geometry* (see especially 111ff.). He discusses his differences from the phenomenology of Merleau-Ponty and Sartre again in his thesis defense, written in 1980 ("Ponctuations" esp. 444). His most sustained critique of Lacan, at times becoming very personal, is "Le facteur de la vérité" (CP 439–524; trans. 411–96).

13. Derrida has, of course, presented his extended analysis of the metaphorical/nonmetaphorical underpinnings of philosophical discourse in "La mythologie blanche" (M 247–324; trans. 207–71). This essay, like *Glas*, is routinely misunderstood in the subsequent critical responses to Derrida as saying something banal like all philosophy relies on metaphor and so is only a subspecies of literary expression.

14. That this position of the nonheterosexual is both "outside" and also in

some sense radically "inside" the heterosexual logic of social morality is a guiding idea for the anthology *Inside / Out*, edited by Diana Fuss.

15. Mark Taylor says, citing *Glas:* "Something always remains that resists the powerful thrust of *Aufhebung*. This remain(s) as an exteriority that can never be completely interiorized; it is ungraspable, inassimilable, indigestible. This exteriority is the *other* exteriority 'without correspondence with the Hegelian concept of exteriority'" (A 290).

16. As Derrida says in *Glas:* "In effect the doctrine of the death penalty assures the passage from the critique of formalism to the position of absolute *Sittlichkeit* [ethics, or social morality]. In an interpretation that is peculiar to him, Hegel again takes up an argumentation at that time rather current, common to Rousseau and Kant for example: *the death penalty is the condition of freedom* [La doctrine de la peine de mort assure en effet le passage de la critique du formalisme à la position de la *Sittlichkeit* absolue. Dans une interprétation qui lui est propre, Hegel reprend une argumentation alors assez courante, commune à Rousseau et à Kant par exemple: *la peine de mort est la condition de la liberté*]" (*Glas* 114a; 99a; my italics).

17. Of course, "sacred" is one of those "primal words" of which Freud was so fond, words capable of bearing antithetical meanings. The person who is sentenced to die is "sacred" because a scapegoat, as René Girard has specifically discussed (see *La violence et le sacré*). This way of viewing the scapegoat (pharmakos) informs Derrida's analysis in "La pharmacie de Platon" (*La dissémination* 69–198; trans. 61–171; see esp. 146ff.; trans. 128ff.).

18. Or, as Derrida says in an interview from 1988: "Those who accuse me of reducing philosophy to literature or to the logic of rhetoric (see for example the last book by Habermas, *The Philosophical Discourse of Modernity*) have visibly and carefully avoided reading me" (*Points de suspension* 231; my translation).

19. "Un texte ne saurait *appartenir* à aucun genre. Tout texte *participe* d'un ou de plusieurs genres, il n'y a pas de texte sans genre, il y a toujours du genre et des genres mais cette participation n'est jamais une appartenance." Derrida calls this a "hypothesis."

20. As Derrida says in his reading of Kafka's text, "Before the Law": "If Kafka's text says all this about literature, the powerful ellipsis it gives us does not entirely belong to literature. The place from which it tells us *about* the laws of literature, the law without which no literary specificity would take shape or substance, this place cannot be simply *interior* to literature [Si le texte de Kafka dit tout cela de la littérature, l'ellipse puissante qu'il nous livre n'appartient pas totalement à la littérature. Le lieu depuis lequel il nous parle *des* lois de la littérature, de la loi sans laquelle aucune spécificité littéraire ne prendrait figure ou consistance, ce lieu ne peut être simplement *intérieur* à la littérature]" ("Préjugés" 132; AL 214).

21. "Cette possibilité structurelle d'être sevrée du référent ou du signifié (donc de la communication et de son contexte) me paraît faire de toute marque, fûtelle orale, un graphème en général, c'est-à-dire, comme nous l'avons vu, la *restance* non-présente d'une marque différentielle coupée de sa prétendue 'production' ou origine. Et j'étendrai même cette loi à toute 'expérence' en général s'il est acquis qu'il n'y a pas d'expérience de *pure* présence mais seulement des chaînes de marques différentielles" (M 378).

22. In the later "Afterword," Derrida offers this further definition of iterability: "What in this context I call iterability is at once that which tends to attain plenitude and that which bars access to it. Through the possibility of repeating every mark as the same it makes way for an idealization that seems to deliver the full presence of ideal objects . . . , but this repeatability itself ensures that the full presence of a singularity thus repeated comports in itself the reference to something else, thus rending the full presence that it nevertheless announces. This is why iteration is not simply repetition" (*Limited Inc* 129).

23. Though this kind of language tends toward the foundationalism of which Rorty accuses Gasché, as we have seen. The use of this kind of term allows Irene Harvey, for example, to describe Derrida's extended sense of "writing" as follows: "The issue is to show the conditions of possibility of *Logos* and hence of truth" (153).

24. Jeffrey Nealon has usefully distinguished between Derrida's use of "undecidability" and Paul de Man's, by saying, in part: "For Derrida, undecidability—the neutralization of oppositions within a generalizing system—entails a distinctly ethical imperative to rethink decision carefully and complexly" (1271). Derrida insists on this ethical aspect of the aporias associated with acts of judgment, as when he says "deconstruction calls for an increase in responsibility" ("Force of Law" 20).

25. "Le danger pour une tâche de déconstruction, ce serait plutôt la *possibilité*, et de devenir un ensemble disponible de procédures réglées, de pratiques méthodiques, de chemins accessibles. L'intérêt de la déconstruction, de sa force et de son désir si elle en a, c'est une certaine expérience de l'impossible: c'est-à-dire . . . *de l'autre*, l'expérience de l'autre comme invention de l'impossible, en d'autres termes comme la seule invention possible" (*Psyché* 26–27). Derrida says something similar in discussing de Man's work: "This is impossible, but no one has ever said that deconstruction, as a technique or a method, was possible; it thinks only on the level of the impossible and of what is still evoked as unthinkable" (*Mémoires* 135).

26. See especially Derrida, *Donner—le temps*.

27. "Le don *n'est pas*, on ne peut demander 'qu-est-ce que le don?' mais c'est à cette *condition* qu'il y aurait eu, sous ce nom ou sous un autre, un don."

28. Charles Altieri has proposed a strong reading of what Derrida means by "singularity" in the context of ethical deconstruction through a comparison with postmodern art in the essay "Frank Stella and Jacques Derrida: Toward a

Postmodern Ethics of Singularity." Singularity is a strong theme in Derrida's meditations on Kierkegaard's *Fear and Trembling*, especially the ethical demand represented by the sacrifice of Isaac, in *Donner la mort*.

29. "L'invention de l'autre, venue de l'autre, cela ne se *construit* certainement pas comme un génitif subjectif, mais pas davantage comme un génitif objectif, même si l'invention vient de l'autre. Car celui-ci, dès lors, n'est ni sujet ni objet, ni un moi, ni une conscience ni un inconscient. *Se préparer à cette venue de l'autre, c'est ce qu'on peut appeler la déconstruction"* (my translation; my italics; passage not in the English translation of "Psyche" [AL]).

30. This kind of thinking informs Lyotard's meditations on "phrasing" in *Lé Différend*.

31. This quest was seen to underlie some of the disagreements between different versions of feminism, in the previous chapter: whether feminism should present prescriptive phrases for change, or whether the ethical challenge is rather to maintain a nonnormative stance allowing for and encouraging difference and radical otherness (see Card, *Feminist Ethics*).

Chapter Seven

1. This oversimplified version of Derrida's position provides a recurring straw man for Don Byrd in his otherwise provocative and illuminating *Poetics of the Common Knowledge* (esp. 60–61; 74–79; 100–101). Byrd, for example, claims that "the poetics of the common knowledge understands 'difference'—the difference that is not identical, in Derrida's formulation[—]as a dimension not of linguistic slippage but of poetic *precision"* (115–16). In the view that emerges more fully in this chapter, I see the latter as a false distinction.

2. This relates to Levinas's philosophical investigation of the "Saying" and the "Said" ("le Dire" and "le Dit") in *Autrement qu'être* (*Otherwise than Being*).

3. I disagree with Simon Critchley's and Robert Bernasconi's view that "Violence and Metaphysics" can be viewed as a self-deconstructive or "double reading" and *not* a critique of Levinas's thought (Critchley, *The Ethics of Deconstruction* 112). A comparison of "At This Very Moment" to the earlier essay shows rather the distance Derrida has traversed in his own thinking as it has developed to bring him closer to the ethical thinking of Levinas.

4. Simon Critchley gives a provocative reading of this passage from "En ce moment même" by taking seriously the idea that the voice speaking here is that of a woman (*The Ethics of Deconstruction* 132–37). The whole question of the gendering of the philosophical discourse leads to some of Derrida's most controversial utterances, for example, his discussion in *Spurs* of the place of "the woman" in Nietzsche's thinking. The strongest recuperative reading of Derrida's *Spurs* from a feminist perspective is that of Drucilla Cornell (see *Transformations* 50). The performance of *Feu la cendre* as a text for male and female voices continues this strain.

5. *"Nombres* inlassablement extraits de la crypte où vous les auriez crus encoffrés. Indéchiffrables parce que c'est seulement dans votre représentation qu'ils prenaient l'aplomb d'un cryptogramme cachant en soi le secret d'un sens ou d'une référence."

6. "Si l'écriture appartient à la *physis*, n'est-ce pas à tel moment de la *physis*, à tel mouvement nécessaire par lequel sa vérité, la production de son apparaître aime, dit Héraclite, à s'abriter en sa crypte? 'Cryptogramme' condense en un seul mot la proposition d'un pléonasme."

7. It helps to recall Lacan's statement: "Car il ne suffit pas d'en décider par son effet: la Mort. Il s'agit encore de savoir quelle mort, celle que porte la vie ou celle qui la porte [Because it is not enough to judge by its effect: Death. It's still a matter of knowing which death, that which life carries or that which carries it]" (E 810; my translation). One could say that Derrida's thinking on the crypt is his way of revisiting this Lacanian topic obliquely.

8. As Derrida says, "Cryptic incorporation always marks the effect of an impossible or refused mourning [l'incorporation cryptique marque toujours un effet de deuil impossible ou refusé]" ("Fors" 25; trans. xxi).

9. "Love/hate" would be a rough translation for Kristeva's important concept of *hainamoration* developed in her *Histoires d'amour.*

10. "Crypter: le verbe, je crois ne l'avoir pas encore utilisé. Crypter, c'est chiffrer, opération symbolique ou sémiotique qui consiste à manipuler un code secret, ce qu'on ne peut jamais faire seul."

11. See, notably, Lacan's discussion of Bernini's Saint Theresa, *Le Séminaire XX: Encore,* which in turn provokes Luce Irigaray's response in her "Cosi fan tutti" (CS 82–101).

12. "Cette fonction *agogique* de conducteur d'hommes, de *duce,* de *Führer,* de *leader* le place au-dessus de la foule qu'il manipule par l'intermédiare *d'un petit nombre d'adeptes rassemblés dans une secte au langage crypté,* une bande, une clique ou un petit parti avec ses pratiques ritualisées" (final italics mine).

13. This is, incidentally, the only element I find missing in Ned Lukacher's otherwise brilliant and searching introduction to his translation of Derrida's *Cinders,* "Mourning Becomes Telepathy."

14. Herman Rapaport's discussion of Derrida's analysis of Heidegger's thinking on *Geist* (Rapaport 155–74) includes such an indication, as when he says: "To this end Western anti-Semitism is conceivable to be a requirement of all the metaphysical institutions of thought, a requirement that Western philosophy has encrypted inside itself even as it has struggled to release itself from that burden" (174).

15. This would be one way to account for the copresence of both hysteria and a strange mood of self-congratulation in many of the writings produced in the wake of the discovery of Paul de Man's early journalism. William V. Spanos has begun to investigate some of these questions in his *Heidegger and Criticism.*

16. William V. Spanos says, in part: "To read Heidegger's texts after the brief period of the rectorship (April 1933-February 1934) in the 'light' of the accomplished enormities of the Nazis would terminate in the repression of the voice of one of the greatest thinkers in the history of Western philosophy. More important, it would constitute a tacit acknowledgment and confirmation of the Western metaphysical tradition: the tradition, according to Heidegger's essential thought, that has come to its end in the globalization of *Technik*. It would, in short, tacitly reprieve the West's essential complicity in the making of the Nazi machine and the horrors it perpetuated" (105).

17. "N'oubliez pas qu'il reste en mémoire de feu, du mot feu dans l'expression feu un tel ou feu une telle [do not forget that it remains in memory of the departed (*feu*—also fire), of the word *feu* in the idiom, 'the late so and so,' the departed, the bereaved]" (*Cinders* 35).

18. As to why ethics is always the *question* of ethics, see Charles E. Scott, *The Question of Ethics* (esp. 1–12).

19. As John D. Caputo phrases this: "Undecidability does not detract from the urgency of decision; it simply underlines the difficulty" (4).

20. Or, as Derrida says in "En ce moment même," "Il n'y aurait pas de langage sans cette responsabilité (éthique) mais il n'*est jamais sûr* que le langage se rende à la responsabilité qui le rend possible [Without that (ethical) responsibility there would be no language, but it *is never sure* that language surrenders itself to the responsibility that makes it possible]" (*Psyché* 174; trans. 23).

Works Cited

Adorno, Theodor W. *Jargon der Eigentlichkeit: Zur deutschen Ideologie.* Frankfurt a.M.: Suhrkamp Verlag, 1964. [*The Jargon of Authenticity.* Trans. Knut Tarnowski and Frederic Will. Evanston, Ill.: Northwestern University Press, 1973.]

Ainley, Alison. "The Ethics of Sexual Difference," in Fletcher and Benjamin, eds., 53–62.

Altieri, Charles. *Canons and Consequences: Reflections on the Ethical Force of Imaginative Ideals.* Evanston, Ill.: Northwestern University Press, 1990.

———. "Frank Stella and Jacques Derrida: Toward a Postmodern Ethics of Singularity," in Brunette and Wills, eds., 168–87.

Baker, Peter. "In Sight of the Mountain" (poem) and "A Place of Sense" (short essay). *Poet and Critic* 14:1 (1983).

———. "Metric, Naming and Exile: Perse/Pound/Genet." In *The Scope of Words: In Honor of Albert S. Cook,* ed. Peter Baker, Sarah Webster Goodwin and Gary Handwerk, 39–58. New York: Peter Lang, 1991.

———. *Modern Poetic Practice: Structure and Genesis.* New York: Peter Lang, 1986.

———. *Obdurate Brilliance: Exteriority and the Modern Long Poem.* Gainesville: University Press of Florida, 1991.

———. "'To disarm the cryptogram': The Languages of Contemporary Poetry." *The Centennial Review* 36:2 (1992): 231–41.

Barzilai, Shuli. "Borders of Language: Kristeva's Critique of Lacan." *PMLA* 106 (1991), 294–305.

Bennington, Geoffrey, and Jacques Derrida. *Jacques Derrida.* Paris: Seuil, 1991. Trans. Geoffrey Bennington. Chicago: University of Chicago Press, 1992.

Benveniste, Emile. *Problèmes de linguistique générale.* Paris: Gallimard, 1966. [*Problems in General Linguistics.* Trans. Mary Elizabeth Meek. Coral Gables: University of Miami Press, 1971.]

Bernasconi, Robert. "Deconstruction and the Possibility of Ethics," in Sallis, ed., 122–39.

―――. "No More Stories, Good or Bad: de Man's Criticisms of Derrida on Rousseau," in Wood, ed., 137–66.

―――. "The Trace of Levinas in Derrida," in Wood and Bernasconi, eds., 13–29.

Bernasconi, Robert, and Simon Critchley, eds. *Re-Reading Levinas*. Bloomington: Indiana University Press, 1991.

Bernstein, Charles. "Artifice of Absorption." In *A Poetics*, 9–89. Cambridge: Harvard University Press, 1992; originally published as an issue of *Paper Air* 4:1 (1987).

Blanchot, Maurice. *L'Entretien infini* [EI]. Paris: Gallimard, 1969.

Bloom, Harold. *The Anxiety of Influence*. New York: Oxford University Press, 1973.

Booth, Wayne. *The Company We Keep: An Ethics of Fiction*. Berkeley: University of California Press, 1988.

Bové, Paul. *In the Wake of Theory*. Hanover, N.H.: Wesleyan University Press/ University Press of New England, 1992.

Brunette, Peter, and David Wills, eds. *Deconstruction and the Visual Arts* [DVA]. Cambridge: Cambridge University Press, 1994.

Buber, Martin. *I and Thou* (1923; rev. 1957). Trans. Walter Kaufman. New York: Scribner's, 1970.

Butler, Judith. *Gender Trouble: Feminism and the Subversion of Identity* [GT]. New York: Routledge, 1990.

―――. "Imitation and Gender Insubordination," in Fuss, ed., 13–31.

Byrd, Don. *The Poetics of the Common Knowledge*. Albany: State University of New York Press, 1994.

Caputo, John D. *Against Ethics*. Bloomington: Indiana University Press, 1993.

Card, Claudia. "The Feistiness of Feminism," in Card, ed., 3–31.

―――, ed. *Feminist Ethics*. Lawrence: University Press of Kansas, 1991.

Céline, Louis-Ferdinand. *Voyage au bout de la nuit* (1932). Paris: Gallimard, 1952.

Chodorow, Nancy. *Feminism and Psychoanalytic Theory*. New Haven: Yale University Press, 1989.

Cixous, Hélène. *Entre l'écriture*. Paris: des femmes, 1986. [*"Coming to Writing" and Other Essays*. Ed. Deborah Jenson. Trans. Sarah Cornell, Deborah Jenson, Ann Liddle, Susan Sellers. Cambridge: Harvard University Press, 1991.]

Clover, Carol J. *Men, Women, and Chain Saws: Gender in the Modern Horror Film*. Princeton: Princeton University Press, 1992.

Cook, Albert. *Canons and Wisdoms*. Philadelphia: University of Pennsylvania Press, 1993.

Cornell, Drucilla. *The Philosophy of the Limit* [PL]. New York: Routledge, 1992.

―――. *Transformations: Recollective Imagination and Sexual Difference*. New York: Routledge, 1993.

Cornell, Drucilla, Michel Rosenfeld, and David Gray Carlson, eds. *Deconstruction and the Possibility of Justice*. New York: Routledge, 1992.

Coward, Harold, and Toby Foshay, eds. *Derrida and Negative Theology* [DNT]. Albany: State University of New York Press, 1992.

Critchley, Simon. "The Chiasmus: Levinas, Derrida and the Ethical Demand for Deconstruction." *Textual Practice* 3:1 (1989), 91–106.

———. *The Ethics of Deconstruction: Derrida and Levinas*. Oxford: Blackwell, 1992.

de Lauretis, Teresa. *Technologies of Gender: Essays on Theory, Film and Fiction*. Bloomington: Indiana University Press, 1987.

Deleuze, Gilles. *Différence et répétition* [DR]. Paris: Presses Universitaires de France, 1967.

———. *Foucault*. Paris: Minuit, 1986.

Deleuze, Gilles, and Felix Guattari. *L'Anti-Oedipe*. Paris: Minuit, 1972.

———. *Mille Plateaux*. Paris: Minuit, 1980.

de Man, Paul. *Allegories of Reading: Figural Language in Rousseau, Nietzsche, Rilke, and Proust*. New Haven: Yale University Press, 1979.

———. *The Resistance to Theory*. Minneapolis: University of Minnesota Press, 1986.

———. *Wartime Journalism*. Lincoln: University of Nebraska Press, 1988.

Derrida, Jacques. *Acts of Literature* [AL]. Ed. Derek Attridge. New York: Routledge, 1992.

———. *L'autre cap*. Paris: Minuit, 1991. [*The Other Heading*. Trans. Pascale-Anne Brault and Michael B. Naas. Bloomington: Indiana University Press, 1992.]

———. *La carte postale: de Socrate à Freud et au-delà* [CP]. Paris: Flammarion, 1980. [*The Post Card*. Trans. Alan Bass. Chicago: University of Chicago Press, 1987.]

———. "Circonfession," in Bennington and Derrida, *Jacques Derrida*.

———. "Comment ne pas parler," in *Psyché*, 535–95. ["How to avoid speaking: Denials (DNT)." Trans. Ken Frieden, in Coward and Foshay, eds., 73–142.]

———. "Deconstruction and the Other" (interview). In *Dialogues with Contemporary Continental Thinkers*, ed. Richard Kearney, 105–26. Manchester, England: Manchester University Press, 1984.

———. "Deconstruction in America" (interview). *Critical Exchange* 17 (1985), 1–33.

———. "La différance," in *Marges* [M], 1–29. ["Différance," in *Margins of Philosophy*, 1–27.]

———. *La dissémination*. Paris: Seuil, 1972. [*Dissemination*. Trans. Barbara Johnson. Chicago: University of Chicago Press, 1981.]

———. *Donner la mort*, in Rabaté and Wetzel, eds., *L'Éthique du don*, 11–108.

———. *Donner—le temps*. Paris: Galilée, 1991. [*Given Time: I. Counterfeit Money*. Trans. Peggy Kamuf. Chicago: University of Chicago Press, 1992.]

———. *Du droit à la philosophie*. Paris: Galilée, 1990.

———. "D'un ton apocalyptique adopté naguère en philosophie." In *Les fins de l'homme*, 445–79. Paris: Galilée, 1981. Paris: Galilée, 1983 [rpt.]. ["On a Newly Arisen Apocalyptic Tone in Philosophy." Trans. John P. Leavey, in *Raising the Tone of Philosophy*, ed. Peter Fenves, 117–71. Baltimore: Johns Hopkins University Press, 1993.]

———. *L'Écriture et la différence* [ED]. Paris: Seuil, 1967. [*Writing and Difference* (WD). Trans. Alan Bass. Chicago: University of Chicago Press, 1978.]

———. *Edmund Husserl's "Origin of Geometry": An Introduction*. Trans. John P. Leavy. Lincoln: University of Nebraska Press, 1989 [rev. ed.]

———. "En ce moment même dans cet ouvrage me voici," in *Psyché* 159–202. ["At This Very Moment in This Work Here I Am." Trans. Ruben Berezdivin, in Bernasconi and Critchley, eds., 11–48.]

———. *Éperons: Les styles de Nietzsche* (1978). [*Spurs: Nietzsche's Styles*. Trans. Barbara Harlow. Chicago: University of Chicago Press, 1979 (bilingual edition).]

———. *Feu la cendre*. Paris: des femmes, 1987. [*Cinders*. Trans. Ned Lukacher. Lincoln: University of Nebraska Press, 1991 (bilingual edition).]

———. "Force of Law: The 'Mystical Foundation of Authority.'" Trans. Mary Quaintance, in Cornell et al., eds., 3–67.

———. "Fors." Foreword to Nicolas Abraham and Maria Torok, *La Cryptonymie: Le verbier de l'homme aux loups*. Paris: Aubier Flammarion, 1976, 7–73. [*The Wolf Man's Magic Word: A Cryptonymy*. Trans. Nicholas Rand, foreword trans. Barbara Johnson. Minneapolis: University of Minnesota Press, 1986.]

———. *Glas* (1974). Paris: Galilée. Paris: Denoël/Gonthier, 1981 (reprint). Trans. John Leavy and Richard Rand. Lincoln: University of Nebraska Press, 1986.

———. *De la grammatologie* [G]. Paris: Minuit, 1967. [*Of Grammatology*. Trans. Gayatri Spivak. Baltimore: Johns Hopkins University Press, 1976.]

———. *Heidegger et la question: De l'esprit et autres essais* [HQ]. Paris: Flammarion, 1990 [*De l'esprit*, originally published by Galilée in 1987]. [*Of Spirit: Heidegger and the Question*. Trans. Geoffrey Bennington and Rachel Bowlby. Chicago: University of Chicago Press, 1989.]

———. "Like the Sound of the Sea Deep within a Shell: Paul de Man's War," in *Mémoires* [rev. ed.], 155–263.

———. *Limited Inc*. Evanston, Ill.: Northwestern University Press, 1988 [rev. ed.].

———. "La loi du genre," in *Parages*, 249–87. ["The Law of Genre." Trans. Avital Ronell, in *Acts of Literature* (AL), 223–52.]

———. *Marges de la philosophie* [M]. Paris: Minuit, 1972. [*Margins of Philosophy*. Trans. Alan Bass. Chicago: University of Chicago Press, 1982.]

———. *Mémoires: For Paul de Man*. New York: Columbia University Press, 1989 [rev. ed.].

———. *Parages*. Paris: Galilée, 1986.

———. *Points de suspension (Entretiens)*. Paris: Galilée, 1992.

———. "Ponctuations: le temps de la thèse." In *Du droit à la philosophie*, 439–59. ["The time of a thesis." In *Philosophy in France Today*, ed. Alan Montefiore, 34–50. Cambridge: Cambridge University Press, 1984.]

———. "Préjugés: devant la loi." In Lyotard et al., *La faculté de juger*, 87–139. Paris: Minuit, 1985. ["Before the Law." Trans. Avital Ronell and Christine Roulston, in *Acts of Literature* (AL), 183–220.]

———. "Psyche: Invention of the Other." Trans. Catherine Porter, in *Acts of Literature* [AL], 311–43.

———. *Psyché: Inventions de l'autre*. Paris: Galilée, 1987.

———. "Les pupilles de l'Université: Le principe de raison et l'idée de l'Université." In *Du droit à la philosophie*, 461–98. ["The Principle of Reason: The University in the Eyes of Its Pupils." *Diacritics* 13 (1983), 3–20.]

———. "Signature événement contexte," in *Marges* [M], 365–93. ["Signature Event Context" (SEC). Trans. Samuel Weber and Jeffrey Mehlman, in *Limited Inc*, 1–23.]

———. "The Spatial Arts: An Interview with Jacques Derrida," in Brunette and Wills, eds., [DVA] 9–32.

———. *La vérité en peinture*. Paris: Flammarion (Champs), 1978. [*The Truth in Painting*. Trans. Geoff Bennington and Ian McLeod. Chicago: University of Chicago Press, 1987.]

———. *La voix et le phénomène: Introduction au problème du signe dans la phénoménologie de Husserl* [VP]. Paris: Presses Universitaires de France, 1967. [*Speech and Phenomena*. Trans. David Allison. Evanston, Ill.: Northwestern University Press, 1973.]

Derrida, Jacques, and Pierre-Jean Labarrière. *Altérités*. Paris: Osiris, 1986.

Descombes, Vincent. *Le Même et l'autre* [MA]. Paris: Minuit, 1979. [*Modern French Philosophy* (MFP). Trans. L. Scott-Fox and J. M. Harding. Cambridge: Cambridge University Press, 1980.]

Diamond, Irene, and Lee Quinby, eds. *Feminism and Foucault: Reflections on Resistance*. Boston: Northeastern University Press, 1988.

Dreyfus, Hubert, and Paul Rabinow. *Michel Foucault: Beyond Structuralism and Hermeneutics*. 2d ed. Chicago: University of Chicago Press, 1983.

Erens, Patricia, ed. *Issues in Feminist Film Criticism*. Bloomington: Indiana University Press, 1990.

Ferry, Luc, and Alain Renaut. *La pensée 68: Essai sur l'antihumanisme contemporain*. Paris: Gallimard, 1985. [*French Philosophy of the Sixties*. Trans. Mary H. S. Cattani. Cambridge: Massachusetts Institute of Technology Press, 1990.]

Fish, Stanley. *Doing What Comes Naturally: Change, Rhetoric and the Practice of Theory in Literary and Legal Studies*. Durham: Duke University Press, 1989.

Fletcher, John, and Andrew Benjamin, eds. *Abjection, Melancholia and Love: The Work of Julia Kristeva*. London and New York: Routledge, 1990.

Foucault, Michel. "Afterword: The Subject and Power," in Dreyfus and Rabinow, 208–26.

———. "The Ethic of Care for the Self as a Practice of Freedom" [ECS]. *Philosophy and Social Criticism* 2–3 (1987), 112–31. (Reprinted in *The Final Foucault*, 1–20.)

———. *The Final Foucault.* Ed. James Bernauer and David Rasmussen. Cambridge: Massachusetts Institute of Technology Press, 1988.

———. *Foucault Live (Interviews 1966–1984).* Ed. Sylvère Lotringer. New York: Semiotext(e), 1989.

———. *The Foucault Reader.* Ed. Paul Rabinow. New York: Pantheon, 1984.

———. *Histoire de la sexualité, La volonté de savoir* [VS]. Paris: Gallimard, 1976. [*The History of Sexuality 1: An Introduction.* Trans. Robert Hurley. New York: Pantheon, 1978.]

———. *Language, Counter-Memory, Practice.* Ed. Donald F. Bouchard. Ithaca: Cornell University Press, 1977.

———. *Les mots et les choses.* Paris: Gallimard, 1966. [*The Order of Things* (1970). New York: Pantheon, 1971.]

———. "Nietzsche, Genealogy, History" [NGH]. In *Language, Counter-Memory, Practice,* 139–64. (French text originally published in *Hommage à Jean Hyppolite,* Paris: Presses Universitaires de France, 1971, 145–72.)

———. *Surveiller et punir: Naissance de la prison.* Paris: Gallimard, 1975. [*Discipline and Punish: The Birth of the Prison.* Trans. Alan Sheridan. New York: Pantheon, 1977.]

———. "What Is Enlightenment?" in *The Foucault Reader,* 32–50.

Frege, Gottlob. "On Sense and Reference" [Über Sinn und Bedeutung] (1892). In *Philosophical Writings,* 56–78. Oxford: Blackwell, 1960.

Fuss, Diana. *Essentially Speaking: Feminism, Nature and Difference.* New York: Routledge, 1989.

———, ed. *Inside / Out: Lesbian Theories, Gay Theories.* New York: Routledge, 1991.

Gallop, Jane. *Reading Lacan.* Ithaca: Cornell University Press, 1985.

Gasché, Rodolphe. *The Tain of the Mirror: Derrida and the Philosophy of Reflection.* Cambridge: Harvard University Press, 1986.

Genet, Jean. *Un captif amoureux.* Paris: Gallimard, 1986.

———. *Miracle de la rose* [MR]. Paris: Marc Barbezat-l'Arbalète, 1946. [*Miracle of the Rose.* Trans. Bernard Frechtman. New York: Grove Press, 1966.]

Gilbert, Sandra, and Susan Gubar. *No Man's Land* (v. I): *The War of the Words.* New Haven: Yale University Press, 1988.

Girard, René. *La violence et le sacré.* Paris: Grasset, 1972.

Habermas, Jürgen. *Der philosophische Diskurs der Moderne: Zwölf Vorlesungen.* Frankfurt a.M.: Suhrkamp Verlag, 1985. [*The Philosophical Discourse of Modernity: Twelve Lectures* (PDM). Trans. Frederick G. Lawrence. Cambridge: Massachusetts Institute of Technology Press, 1987.]

Hadreas, Peter J. *In Place of the Flawed Diamond: An Investigation of Merleau-Ponty's Philosophy.* New York: Peter Lang, 1986.

Hamacher, Werner. "LECTIO: de Man's Imperative." Trans. Susan Bernstein, in Waters and Godzich, eds., 171–201.

Handwerk, Gary. "The Irony of Double Vision: Lacan's Liquidation of the Subject." In *Irony and Ethics in Narrative*, 125–71. New Haven: Yale University Press, 1985.

Harpham, Geoffrey Galt. "Derrida and the Ethics of Criticism." *Textual Practice* 5:3 (1991), 383–98.

———. "Language, History and Ethics." *Raritan* 7:1 (1987), 128–46.

Hartman, Geoffrey. *Saving the Text: Literature, Derrida, Philosophy.* Baltimore: Johns Hopkins University Press, 1981.

Harvey, Irene E. *Derrida and the Economy of "Différance."* Bloomington: Indiana University Press, 1986.

Hegel, G. W. F. *Philosophy of Right* (1965). Trans. T. M. Knox. Oxford: Oxford University Press, 1967.

Heidegger, Martin. *Being and Time.* Trans. J. Macquarrie and E. Robinson. New York: Harper and Row, 1962.

———. "Language in the Poem: A Discussion of Georg Trakl's Poetic Work." In *On the Way to Language.* Trans. Peter D. Hertz. New York: Harper and Row, 1971. (Originally published as "Die Sprache im Gedicht, Eine Erörterung von Georg Trakls Gedicht," in *Unterwegs zur Sprache*; Pfullingen: Neske, 1959.)

———. "Poetically Man Dwells." In *Poetry Language Thought.* Trans. Albert Hofstadter. New York: Harper and Row, 1971. (Originally published in *Vorträge und Aufsätze*; Pfullingen: Günther Neske, 1954.)

———. "The Principle of Identity" ["Der Satz der Identität"]. 1957 lecture. In *Identity and Difference* [ID] (bilingual text). Trans. Joan Stambaugh. New York: Harper and Row, 1969. (Originally published as *Identität und Differenz*; Pfullingen: Günther Neske, 1957.)

Hill, Leslie. "Julia Kristeva: Theorizing the Avant-Garde?" In Fletcher and Benjamin, eds., 137–56.

Irigaray, Luce. *Ce sexe qui n'en est pas un* [CS]. Paris: Minuit, 1977. [*This Sex Which Is Not One.* Trans. Catherine Porter with Carolyn Burke. Ithaca: Cornell University Press, 1985.]

———. *Éthique de la différence sexuelle* [EDS]. Paris: Minuit, 1984.

Jaggar, Alison M. "Feminist Ethics: Projects, Problems, Projects," in Card, ed., 78–104.

Jardine, Alice. *Gynesis: Configurations of Woman and Modernity.* Ithaca: Cornell University Press, 1985.

———. "Opaque Texts and Transparent Contexts: The Political Difference of Julia Kristeva" [OT]. In *The Poetics of Gender*, ed. Nancy K. Miller, 96–116. New York: Columbia University Press, 1986.

Kempley, Rita. Review of *The Silence of the Lambs*. *Washington Post*, February 15, 1991, C1.

Kierkegaard, Søren. *Fear and Trembling*. Trans. Howard V. Hong and Edna H. Hong. Princeton: Princeton University Press, 1983.

Kristeva, Julia. *Des chinoises*. Paris: des femmes, 1977. [*About Chinese Women*. Trans. Anita Barrows. London: Marion Boyars, 1977.]

———. *Histoires d'amour* [HA]. Paris: Denoël, 1983. [*Tales of Love* (TL). Trans. Leon S. Roudiez. New York: Columbia University Press, 1987.]

———. *Pouvoirs de l'horreur* [PH]. Paris: Seuil, 1980. [*Powers of Horror*. Trans. Leon S. Roudiez. New York: Columbia University Press, 1982.]

———. *La révolution du langage poétique* [RLP]. Paris: Seuil, 1974. [*Revolution in Poetic Language*. Trans. Margaret Waller, New York: Columbia University Press, 1984.]

———. *Soleil noir: Dépression et mélancholie*. Paris: Seuil [Coll. Folio Essais], 1987. [*Black Sun: Depression and Melancholia*. Trans. Leon S. Roudiez. New York: Columbia University Press, 1989.]

———. "Women's Time" [WT]. In *The Kristeva Reader*, ed. Toril Moi, 187–213. Trans. Alice Jardine and Harry Blake. New York: Columbia University Press, 1986. First published in *Signs* 7:1 (1981), 13–35. Originally published as "Le temps des femmes." *Cahiers de recherche de sciences des textes et documents* 5 (1979): 5–19.

Lacan, Jacques. *Écrits* [E]. Paris: Seuil, 1966.

———. "Maurice Merleau-Ponty" [TM]. *Les Temps modernes* 17 (1961), 245–54. Trans. Wilfried Ver Ecke and Dirk de Shutter, in various authors [REPP], 73–82.

———. *Le Séminaire VII: L'éthique de la psychanalyse* [VII]. Paris: Seuil, 1986.

———. *Le Séminaire XI: Les quatre concepts fondamentaux de la psychanalyse* [XI]. Paris: Seuil, 1973. [*The Four Fundamental Concepts of Psycho-Analysis* (FF). Trans. Alan Sheridan. New York: Norton, 1977.]

———. *Le Séminaire XX: Encore*. Paris: Seuil, 1975.

Lacoue-Labarthe, Philippe. *La fiction du politique: Heidegger, l'art et la politique*. Paris: C. Bourgois, 1987. [*Heidegger, Art and Politics*. Trans. Chris Turner. Oxford: Blackwell, 1990.]

Leavy, John P., et al. *Glassary*. Lincoln: University of Nebraska Press, 1986.

Lechte, John. "Art, Love, and Melancholy in the Work of Julia Kristeva," in Fletcher and Benjamin, eds., 24–41.

———. *Julia Kristeva*. London and New York: Routledge, 1990.

Levanture, Albert, with Thomas Keenan. "A Bibliography of the Works of Jacques Derrida," in Wood, ed., 247–89.

Levinas, Emmanuel. *L'autrement qu'être ou au-delà de l'essence*. Dordrecht: Kluwer, 1978. [*Otherwise than Being or beyond Essence*. Trans. Alphonso Lingis. The Hague: Martinus Nijhoff, 1981.]

———. *Totalité et infini: essai sur l'extériorité* [TI]. The Hague: Martinus Nijhoff, 1961 (3d ed. 1968). [*Totality and Infinity: An Essay on Exteriority.* Trans. Alphonso Lingis. Pittsburgh: Duquesne University Press, 1969.]

Llewelyn, John. *Derrida on the Threshold of Sense.* New York: St. Martin's, 1986.

Lukacher, Ned. "Mourning Becomes Telepathy" (translator's introduction), in Derrida, *Cinders,* 1–18.

Lyotard, Jean-François. *La condition postmoderne* [CP]. Paris: Minuit, 1979. [*The Postmodern Condition.* Trans. Geoff Bennington and Brian Massumi. Minneapolis: University of Minnesota Press, 1984.]

———. *Le Différend* [D]. Paris: Minuit, 1983. Trans. Georges Van Den Abbeele. Minneapolis: University of Minnesota Press, 1988.

———. *Discours, figure* [DF]. Paris: Klincksieck, 1971.

———. "Histoire universelle et différences culturelles." *Critique* 456 (1981), 559–68. ["Universal History and Cultural Differences." Trans. David Macey. In *The Lyotard Reader,* ed. Andrew Benjamin, 314–23. Oxford: Blackwell, 1989.]

———. *La phénoménologie.* Paris: Presses Universitaires de France, 1954.

Madison, Gary Brent. *The Phenomenology of Merleau-Ponty.* Athens: Ohio University Press, 1981.

Marcus, Sharon. "Fighting Bodies, Fighting Words: A Theory and Politics of Rape Prevention." In *Feminists Theorize the Political,* ed. Judith Butler and Joan W. Scott, 385–403. New York: Routledge, 1992.

Maslin, Janet. "Lay Off *Thelma and Louise.*" *New York Times,* June 16, 1991: H11, H16.

"Maurice Merleau-Ponty and Psychology." Special issue, *Review of Existential Psychology and Psychiatry* [REPP] 18 (1982–83), 1–3.

Meese, Elizabeth. *Crossing the Double-Cross: The Practice of Feminist Criticism.* Chapel Hill: University of North Carolina Press, 1986.

———. *(Ex)Tensions: Refiguring Feminist Criticism.* Urbana: University of Illinois Press, 1990.

Merleau-Ponty, Maurice. *L'Oeil et l'Esprit* [OE]. Paris: Gallimard, 1964. ["Eye and Mind" (EM). Trans. Carleton Dallery. In *The Primacy of Perception,* 159–190. Evanston, Ill.: Northwestern University Press, 1978.]

———. *La Phénoménologie de la perception* [PP]. Paris: Gallimard [Coll. Tel], 1945. [*The Phenomenology of Perception.* Trans. Colin Smith. New York: Humanities Press, 1962.]

———. *Le Visible et l'invisible* [VI]. Ed. Claude Lefort. Paris: Gallimard [Coll. Tel], 1964. [*The Visible and the Invisible.* Trans. Alphonso Lingis. Evanston, Ill.: Northwestern University Press, 1968.]

Miller, J. Hillis. "Derrida's Topographies." *South Atlantic Review* 59:9 (1994), 1–25.

———. *The Ethics of Reading.* New York: Columbia University Press, 1987.

Moi, Toril. *Sexual/Textual Politics: Feminist Literary Theory.* London and New York: Methuen, 1985.

Mulvey, Laura. "Visual Pleasure and Narrative Cinema." *Screen* 16:3 (1975), 6–18. Reprinted in Erens, ed., 28–40.

Nealon, Jeffrey T. "The Discipline of Deconstruction." *PMLA* 107:5 (1992), 1266–79.

Norris, Christopher. *The Contest of the Faculties: Philosophy and Theory after Deconstruction.* London: Methuen, 1985.

———. *Derrida.* Cambridge: Harvard University Press, 1987.

———. *Paul de Man: Deconstruction and the Critique of Aesthetic Ideology.* New York: Routledge, 1988.

———. *Spinoza and the Origins of Modern Critical Theory.* Oxford: Blackwell, 1991.

———. *What's Wrong with Postmodernism: Critical Theory and the Ends of Philosophy* [WWP]. Baltimore: Johns Hopkins University Press, 1990.

O'Connor, Noreen. "An An-Arche of Psychotherapy," in Fletcher and Benjamin, eds., 42–52.

Oliver, Kelly. *Reading Kristeva: Unraveling the Double-bind.* Bloomington: Indiana University Press, 1993.

Plato. *The Collected Dialogues of Plato.* Ed. Edith Hamilton and Huntington Cairns. Princeton: Princeton University Press, 1961.

Poster, Mark. *Critical Theory and Poststructuralism.* Ithaca: Cornell University Press, 1989.

Rabaté, Jean-Michel, and Michael Wetzel, eds. *L'Éthique du don: Jacques Derrida et la pensée du don.* Paris: Métailié-Transition, 1992.

Ragland-Sullivan, Ellie. *Jacques Lacan and the Philosophy of Psychoanalysis.* Urbana: University of Illinois Press, 1986.

Rajchman, John. *Michel Foucault: The Freedom of Philosophy* [MF]. New York: Columbia University Press 1985.

———. *Truth and Eros: Foucault, Lacan and the Question of Ethics* [TE]. New York: Routledge, 1991.

Rapaport, Herman. *Heidegger and Derrida: Reflections on Time and Language.* Lincoln: University of Nebraska Press, 1989.

Rich, Adrienne. "Compulsory Heterosexuality and Lesbian Existence." *Signs* 5:4 (1980), 631–60.

Ronell, Avital. *Crack Wars: Literature Addiction Mania.* Lincoln: University of Nebraska Press, 1992.

Rorty, Richard. *Contingency, Irony, and Solidarity* [CIS]. Cambridge: Cambridge University Press, 1989.

———. *Essays of Heidegger and Others (Philosophical Papers v. II).* Cambridge: Cambridge University Press, 1991.

————. "Is Derrida a Transcendental Philosopher?" *Philosophical Papers* 2: 119–28. Reprinted in Wood, ed., 235–46.

————. "Two Meanings of Logocentrism: A Reply to Norris." *Philosophical Papers* 2: 107–18.

Rose, Jacqueline. *Sexuality in the Field of Vision.* London: Verso, 1986.

Said, Edward W. *The World, the Text, and the Critic.* Cambridge: Harvard University Press, 1983.

Sallis, John, ed. *Deconstruction and Philosophy: The Texts of Jacques Derrida.* Chicago: University of Chicago Press, 1987.

Sartre, Jean-Paul. *L'Etre et le néant.* Paris: Gallimard [Coll. Tel], 1943.

————. *Saint Genet: comédien et martyr.* Paris: Gallimard, 1952.

Schmidt, James. *Maurice Merleau-Ponty: Between Phenomenology and Structuralism.* New York: St. Martin's, 1985.

Scholes, Robert. *Protocols of Reading.* New Haven: Yale University Press, 1989.

Scott, Charles E. *The Question of Ethics: Nietzsche, Foucault, Heidegger.* Bloomington: Indiana University Press, 1990.

Searle, John. "Reiterating the Differences: A Reply to Derrida." *Glyph* 1 (1977), 198–208.

Sichère, Bernard. *Merleau-Ponty: Ou le corps de la philosophie.* Paris: Grasset, 1982.

Smith, Paul. *Discerning the Subject.* Minneapolis: University of Minnesota Press, 1988.

Spanos, William V. *Heidegger and Criticism: Retrieving the Cultural Politics of Destruction.* Minneapolis: University of Minnesota Press, 1993.

Staten, Henry. *Wittgenstein and Derrida.* Lincoln: University of Nebraska Press, 1984.

Stewart, Harry E. "Toward a New Chronology: Jean Genet's Life and Works in 1939." *French Review* 61:1 (1987), 60–64.

Taylor, Mark C. *Altarity* [A]. Chicago: University of Chicago Press, 1987.

————. *Erring: a Postmodern A/theology* [E]. Chicago: University of Chicago Press, 1984.

————. "Introduction: System . . . Structure . . . Difference . . . Other." In *Deconstruction in Context* [DC], ed. Mark Taylor, 1–34. Chicago: University of Chicago Press, 1986.

————. *Tears.* Albany: State University of New York Press, 1990.

Titian, Prince of Painters (exhibition catalogue). Venice: Marsilio Editori, 1990.

Waters, Lindsay, and Wlad Godzich, eds. *Reading de Man Reading.* Minneapolis: University of Minnesota Press, 1989.

White, Edmund. *Genet: A Biography.* New York: Knopf, 1993.

Wittgenstein, Ludwig. *The Blue and Brown Books.* New York: Harper and Row, 1958.

———. *Philosophical Investigations.* Trans. G. E. M. Anscombe, New York: Macmillan, 1958.

———. *Remarks on Colour.* Ed. G. E. M. Anscombe. Trans. Linda McAlister and Margarete Schattle. Berkeley: University of California Press, 1977.

———. *Tractatus Logico-Philosophicus.* Trans. D. F. Pears and B. F. McGuiness. London: Routledge, Kegan Paul, 1961.

———. *Zettel.* Ed. G. E. M. Anscombe and G. H. von Wright. Trans. G. E. M. Anscombe. Oxford: Blackwell, 1967 [rpt. 1970].

Wood, David, ed. *Derrida: A Critical Reader.* Oxford: Blackwell, 1992.

——— and Robert Bernasconi, eds. *Derrida and Différance.* Evanston, Ill.: Northwestern University Press, 1988.

Žižek, Slavoj. *Enjoy Your Symptom! Jacques Lacan in Hollywood and Out.* New York: Routledge, 1992.

Index

163